LUCENT LIBRARY *of* HISTORICAL ERAS

THE UNHOLY CRUSADE:
THE RANSACKING OF MEDIEVAL CONSTANTINOPLE

LUCENT LIBRARY *of* HISTORICAL ERAS

THE UNHOLY CRUSADE:
THE RANSACKING OF MEDIEVAL CONSTANTINOPLE

LUCENT LIBRARY of HISTORICAL ERAS

THE UNHOLY CRUSADE:
THE RANSACKING OF MEDIEVAL CONSTANTINOPLE

WILLIAM W. LACE

LUCENT BOOKS

An imprint of Thomson Gale, a part of The Thomson Corporation

THOMSON

GALE

Detroit • New York • San Francisco • San Diego • New Haven, Conn. • Waterville, Maine • London • Munich

LIBRARY OF CONGRESS CATALOGING-IN-PUBLICATION DATA

Lace, William W.
  The unholy crusade : The ransacking of medieval Constantinople / by William W. Lace.
    p. cm.— (The Lucent library of historical eras. The Middle Ages)
  Includes bibliographical references and index.
  ISBN 1-59018-846-2 (alk. paper)
  1. Crusades—Fourth, 1202–1204—Juvenile literature. 2. Istanbul (Turkey)—History—Siege, 1203–1204—Juvenile literature. I. Title. II. Series: Lucent library of historical eras. Middle Ages.
  D164.L33 2006
  949.5'03—dc22
                                                          2006002572

Printed in China

Contents

Foreword

Looking back from the vantage point of the present, history can be viewed as a myriad of intertwining roads paved by human events. Some paths stand out—broad highways whose mileposts, even from a distance of centuries, are clear. The events that propelled the rise to power of Germany's Third Reich, its role in World War II, and its eventual demise, for example, are well defined and documented.

Other roads are less distinct, their route sometimes hidden from view. Modern legislatures may have developed from old tribal councils, for example, but the links between them are indistinct in places, open to discussion and interpretation.

The architecture of civilization—law, religion, art, science, and government—as well as the more everyday aspects of our culture—what we eat, what we wear—all developed along the historical roads and byways. In that progression can be traced every facet of modern life.

A broad look back along these roads reveals that many paths—though of vastly different character—seem to converge at a few critical junctions. These intersections are those great historical eras that echo over the long, steady course of human history, extending beyond the past and into the present.

These epic periods of time are the focus of Lucent's Library of Historical Eras. They shine through the mists of history like beacons, illuminated by a burst of creativity that propels events forward—so bright that we, from thousands of years away, can clearly see the chain of events leading to the present.

Each Lucent Library of Historical Eras consists of a set of books that highlight various aspects of these major eras. For example, the Elizabethan England library features volumes on Queen Elizabeth I and her court, Elizabethan theater, the great playwrights, and everyday life in Elizabethan London.

The mini-library approach allows for the division of each era into its most significant and most interesting parts and the exploration of those parts in depth. Also, social and cultural trends as well as illustrative documents and eyewitness accounts can be prominently featured in individual volumes.

Lucent's Library of Historical Eras presents a wealth of information to young readers. The lively narrative, fully documented primary and secondary source quotations, maps, photographs, sidebars, and annotated bibliographies serve as launching points for class discussion and further research.

In studying the great historical eras, students also develop a better understanding of our own times. What we learn from the past and how we apply it in the present may shape the future and may determine whether our era will be a guiding light to those traveling future roads.

Introduction

EAST AND WEST

As a new century dawned in the year 1200, Constantinople stood as the most magnificent and cultured city in Christendom, if not in the entire world—enriched by almost nine hundred years of uninterrupted prosperity and by its legacy as the focal point of Christianity in the Middle East. Four years later, much of that magnificence lay in ruins, lost in a three-day rampage of looting and violence.

The despoilers of the city were not the forces of Islam that had already stripped away much of the once-mighty empire of which Constantinople was the capital. Instead, they were fellow Christians, members of the Fourth Crusade, who, after vowing to come to the aid of Christianity in the East, dealt it, historian W.B. Bartlett writes, "a hammer blow from which it would never recover."[1]

The clash between East and West was not the consequence of a sudden rush of events. Rather it was the culmination of centuries of growing suspicion, misperception, and disrespect between two cultures that, while they shared the same religion, shared very little else.

Founding of Constantinople

The East-West divide began in A.D. 330 when Emperor Constantine, having secured sole sovereignty over the vast empire stretching from Persia to Scotland, moved his capital from Rome east to the city of Byzantium, which he renamed for himself—Constantinople. The empire remained under a single ruler only until 395, when it was divided between

Emperor Constantine (in laurel crown) directs the plan for building Constantinople in this seventeenth-century tapestry.

the sons of Theodosius I. From that time on, East and West went their separate ways, never to be reunited.

The Eastern, or Byzantine, Empire prospered, and Constantinople soon became a city of splendor and wealth, far outshining Rome, the Western Empire's capital. Indeed, the once-proud realm of the Caesars found itself increasingly unable to fend off invasions by the wild Germanic tribes from the north. Finally, in 476, the last emperor of the West was forced from his throne and Rome fell to the Ostrogoths.

Religious Differences

The division between East and West, however, was always more theological than territorial or economic. The Eastern, or Orthodox, church was headed by five patriarchs, among whom the patriarch of Constantinople was considered senior. Great councils attended by all these leaders were convened to reach major decisions on doctrine.

The Western church, meanwhile, was governed by one man, the pope, who eventually had absolute rule in matters of faith. His authority, however, did not extend to the East. The patriarchs regarded the pope as their equal and therefore someone to be respected, but not necessarily obeyed. The most bitter quarrels between the two Christian empires came when popes tried to intervene in Byzantine affairs.

Such an event occurred in 867 when the patriarch of Constantinople, Ignatius,

was ousted by a rival named Photius. When Pope Nicholas I supported Ignatius and ordered Photius to step down, the latter responded by excommunicating the pope and all Western clergy, a move that officially cut them off from the entire spiritual life of the church. Photius cited as signs of their heresy the various differences in practice—celibacy of priests, use of unleavened bread at Communion, a slight rewording of the basic creed—that had developed over the centuries.

The breach was eventually smoothed over, but another, more serious split occurred two centuries later when the patriarch of Constantinople, Michael Cerularius, attempted to enforce religious uniformity throughout the East by shutting down churches in the East that catered to Western visitors. The pope, Leo IX, sent an ambassador, Cardinal Humbert, to try to settle the differences. Humbert, instead of trying to negotiate with the patriarch, demanded that the Orthodox church acknowledge the supremacy of the pope. Cerularius refused, and the two traded insults.

On June 6, 1054, Humbert marched up to the high altar of the great church of Hagia Sophia and slapped down a document that, in the pope's name, excommunicated Cerularius as a heretic. Cerularius responded by convening a council that excommunicated the pope. The split between Catholic and Orthodox Christianity was so severe that it remains unhealed more than 950 years later.

Cerularius (left), shown here with Pope Leo IX, was excommunicated from the Western church in 1054. He responded by excommunicating the pope from the Orthodox church.

Trading Ties

Even as East and West drew apart in religion, however, they grew closer in trade. Starting about A.D. 1100, the early Crusades, meant to free the Holy Land from Muslim control, also opened up a vast market in Western Europe for goods from the Middle East and Asia. Most of the trade funneled through Constantinople, and Western merchants —mainly from the great Italian city-states of Pisa, Genoa, and Venice—established trade centers there.

Despite the common goal of making money, it was an uneasy situation. The Westerners and the Byzantines came from different cultures, and neither had much respect for the other. The Byzantines considered the Westerners, whom they called "Latins," barbarians and considered themselves the true heirs of the Roman Empire and often referred to themselves as "Romans." The Europeans thought the Byzantines, whom they called "Greeks," were lazy and degenerate, their glory largely a thing of the past and their military weak, since it was dependent on European mercenaries.

The atmosphere of religious intolerance, economic rivalry, and cultural incompatibility provided more than sufficient fuel for a conflagration. The spark to touch it off would come from the Crusades.

◆ Chapter One

"GOD WILLS IT!"

Even though relations between Byzantium and Western Europe were strained throughout much of the early Middle Ages, the hostilities were largely at arm's length, with rival religious leaders hurling excommunications at each other. That changed dramatically when the first of many Crusades brought the divergent cultures into close contact. And, in one of history's great ironies, it was the Byzantines who sowed the seeds of their own destruction at the hands of the warriors of the Fourth Crusade.

In 1095, Byzantine emperor Alexius I faced an unprecedented threat. Although he had successfully repelled incursions on several fronts, his forces were stretched thin—too thin to withstand a new enemy, the Seljuk Turks, who had managed to capture large chunks of territory. Alexius sent ambassadors to Pope Urban II asking for help.

He would get much more than he bargained for.

Urban's response was to preach a sermon at a great church council in the French city of Clermont. Muslim invaders, he said, were threatening the holiest places in Christendom. Christians of the West must come to the aid of their brothers in the East. They must stop their fighting with each other and join forces against the "infidel."

Urban concluded, according to contemporary accounts, by thundering "Deus vult!" ("God wills it!") The crowd took up the phrase, and it became the rallying cry for the series of holy wars that was to be known as the Crusades.

Preparations

As would always be the case, many months passed from the time the First Crusade was called until armies actually

set out for Palestine. One reason for the delay was that crusaders often had to make as many arrangements for the affairs they left behind as for what lay ahead. Although ordinary soldiers could leave their families and few possessions in the care of relatives, the knights and nobles had to make sure their estates were secure. It was a very genuine concern, for despite threats of legal retribution from the state and eternal damnation from the church, landowners who stayed behind sometimes enriched themselves at the expense of their crusading neighbors.

As well as making arrangements at home, departing crusaders had to fund their own journey. In addition to horses, armor, and weapons, the crusading knight had to have enough money for provisions for both men and horses along the way. It was an extremely expensive enterprise for the members of the nobility. They had to provide not only for themselves, but for the servants and ordinary soldiers who followed them.

All in all, the average knight would be expected to raise about four times his annual income. Where did he get the money? Many had to sell or mortgage some of their lands, but to whom? Not their fellow knights, most of whom were trying to raise money themselves. The only institution with ready cash was the church. In this way, the Crusades, intended to save Christianity in the East, wound up enriching the church in the West in the form of large tracts of land.

The Journey

Once outfitted and assembled, the crusaders faced a formidable journey—more than 2,000 miles (3,200km) from Paris to Jerusalem in an age when most people never traveled more than a few days' walk from where they had been born. Most crusading armies favored the overland route—south along the Rhine River through the German states of Lorraine and Swabia, east along the Danube River through the Balkans, south to Constantinople, across what is now central Turkey, then along the Mediterranean coast through Syria to Palestine.

Travel by sea was shorter both in distance and time, but presented logistical problems, especially the transporting of horses. In any case, the crusaders were landsmen with little liking for ships. Travel by river was one thing; the open sea, subject to sudden violent storms, was another. One French knight, Jean of Joinville, would later write of his sea voyage that he made it a point to say his prayers every night "for what can a voyager tell, when he goes to sleep at night, whether he may be lying at the bottom of the sea the next morning."[2]

Pope Urban II preaches the First Crusade from the pulpit during the Council of Clermont in 1095. Urban's command, "God wills it!" became the crusaders' rallying cry.

Signs from Above

In 1101 German historian Ekkehard of Aurach wrote a history of the world, including an account of the First Crusade. He wrote that some people, in addition to heeding appeals from the pope and other churchmen, were influenced to go on the crusade by heavenly and supernatural signs:

Moreover the signs in the sun and the wonders which appeared, both in the air and on the earth, aroused many who had previously been indifferent. . . . Some . . . reported that they had seen the image of a city in the air and had observed how various troops from different directions, both on horseback and on foot, were hastening thither. Many, moreover, displayed, either on their clothing, or upon their forehead, or elsewhere on their body, the sign of the cross, which had been divinely imprinted. Others likewise were induced, through some sudden change of spirit or some nocturnal vision, to sell all their property and possessions and to sew the sign of mortification on their mantles. . . . I may also report that at this time a woman after two years gestation finally gave birth to a boy who was able to talk; and that a child with a double set of limbs, another with two heads, and some lambs with two heads were also born; and that colts came into the world with great teeth, which we ordinarily call horses' teeth and which nature only grants to three-year-old horses.

Ekkehard of Aurach, *On the Opening of the First Crusade*, in *Internet Medieval Sourcebook*, Paul Halsall, editor. www.fordham.edu/halsall/source/ekkehard-aur1.html.

Reasons for Going

Given the physical and financial hardships, plus the emotional distress of separation from their families, one might reasonably ask why men undertook the Crusades. Religious zeal certainly was a major factor. European Christians in the Middle Ages believed deeply and passionately that, as Urban II said, it was God's will that the Holy Land be reconquered. Contemporary accounts of the Crusades are full of stories about grizzled, hard-bitten warriors shedding copious tears as they pinned red crosses, symbolic of the crusader's vow to fight for Jesus Christ, to their shoulders.

However, it was an age of extreme violence as well as piety. Warfare was a way of life, especially for the nobility, and the entire socioeconomic system known as feudalism was based on military service. Pope Urban's genius was that he was able to link lust for battle with service to the church, thus directing the violence away from Europe and toward a common enemy.

Combat, wherever and against whomever, was also a chance to gain fame and glory. This was especially important to the nobility, where a man's worth was often judged chiefly by his skill as a warrior. English historian and monk William of Malmesbury wrote of the leaders of the First Crusade, "Nothing to be compared with their glory has ever been begotten by any age."[3]

But glory, however important, did not completely justify the tremendous expense involved in crusading. Many knights doubtless traveled eastward seeking fortune as well as fame. Few had been there, but all probably had heard about the opulence of cities such as Damascus and Jerusalem. Where there was fighting, many reasoned, there was bound to be plunder.

Some crusaders had ambitions beyond merely grabbing all the loot they could carry off. There was land to be had as well; knights saw the chance to become counts, and counts the chance to become kings. The opportunity for advancement would have appealed especially to men who had older brothers,

The pope blesses the crusaders as they set sail. Most crusading armies marched overland rather than going to the Holy Land by sea.

Peter the Hermit

Before kings and nobles could respond to Pope Urban II's call for a crusade in 1095, a charismatic figure known as Peter the Hermit gathered a throng of common people and poor knights and headed for Palestine. This account of how he came to lead the People's Crusade is by the twelfth-century German chronicler Albert of Aix:

A certain priest named Peter . . . hearing also that the Patriarch of the city [Jerusalem] was a devout and God-fearing man, he wished to confer with him and to learn more fully from him the truth concerning some matters. . . . [The patriarch] began to disclose to him more confidentially all the evils which the people of God had suffered [at the hands of the Muslims] while dwelling in Jerusalem. To whom Peter replied: "You may be assured, holy father, that if the Roman church and the princes of the West should learn from a zealous and a reliable witness the calamities which you suffer, there is not the slightest doubt that they would hasten to remedy the evil, both by words and deeds. Write them zealously both to the lord Pope and the Roman church and to the kings and princes of the West, and confirm your letter by the authority of your seal. I, truly, for the sake of the salvation of my soul, do not hesitate to undertake this task." [Peter then] proceeded to Rome, and found the lord Pope Urban in the vicinity. He presented the letters of the Patriarch and of the Christians who dwelt at Jerusalem, and showed their misery and the abominations which the unclean races wrought in the holy places. Thus faithfully and prudently he performed the commission entrusted to him.

Quoted in *Peter the Hermit and the Popular Crusade: Collected Accounts*, in *Internet Medieval Sourcebook*, Paul Halsall, editor. www.fordham.edu/halsall/source/peter-hermit. html#tyre.

Peter the Hermit led the first group of warriors to Palestine in the People's Crusade.

since their chances of inheriting titles or property at home were limited at best.

The People's Crusade

However eager most nobles might have been to set out on the First Crusade, it would be nine months before they actually did so. Others, however, had not waited. The pope had called for all people, rich and poor, to take up the cause, and two individuals—a poor knight known as Walter the Penniless and a hermit named Peter—took him at his word.

Walter and a few thousand followers reached Constantinople first and were greeted by Emperor Alexius, although he doubtless was expecting a far greater force. In fact, the greater force was on its way—a large but ragtag army of about twenty thousand led by Peter the Hermit.

Like those who would come after, Walter and Peter had to feed their troops. Walter evidently was not as poor as his name suggests. With one exception, he seems to have been able to buy provisions along the way. Peter, likewise, was able to march through Germany and Hungary without incident until he reached the town of Semlin, which was on the Danube in the westernmost part of the Byzantine Empire.

Semlin was where Walter had encountered trouble. Sixteen of his soldiers had been caught stealing, and the citizens stripped them of their armor, nailing it to the town walls as a warning to the rest of the army. The armor was still in view when Peter approached, and he heeded the warning, trying to lead his troops quickly past the town. Trouble started when the local citizens with supplies to sell began to bargain with Peter's men. An argument broke out that quickly became a battle. The crusaders sacked the town, slaughtering hundreds of citizens and Byzantine troops.

Not content with having stormed one Christian town, the mob crossed the Danube and fell upon the much larger city of Belgrade. The residents, however, had fled eastward, and Peter's troops satisfied themselves by looting the city.

Trouble at Constantinople

Word of these incidents traveled quickly, so when Peter's army joined that of Walter at Constantinople, Emperor Alexius was already fully aware of the danger this motley crowd of foreigners posed to his people. He refused them entry into the city, setting up a market for them outside the walls. Here, they had to buy provisions at what they considered outrageous prices, so instead they began to ravage the surrounding countryside. Before more trouble could erupt, Alexius ferried the crusaders across the narrow strait known as the Bosporus and into Asia.

Peter wanted to wait there for the main body of crusaders that Alexius had told him was coming. His army, however, moved out on its own, ravaging Christian towns as it drove deeper into the interior. In the end, it was lured into an ambush by Turkish troops and massacred. Most of the survivors were sold into slavery, and only about three thousand members of the so-called People's Crusade made it back to Constantinople.

The People's Crusade achieved nothing militarily except perhaps to make the Turks overconfident when they faced the main body of crusaders later on. The People's Crusade did, however, establish an enduring animosity between the Byzantines and the crusaders. The Byzantines considered the crusaders to be ruthless barbarians, caring little if those they killed and plundered were Christian or Muslim. The crusaders considered the Byzantines ungrateful rascals out to swindle and cheat those who had come to fight for God.

The Princes' Crusade

The main body of the First Crusade—called the Princes' Crusade to differentiate it from the unruly mob that had gone before—finally set out early in 1097. Unlike the People's Crusade, its passage through Europe was marked by violence, the most notable targets of which were Jews. The crusaders, in their zeal to fight those they considered enemies of Christianity, made no distinction between the Jews in German cities and the Muslims they had set out to fight in the first place. Many Jewish communities were almost wiped out. Nothing more exemplified the crusaders' curious mixture of religious fervor and stark brutality than did these outrages committed long before they reached the Holy Land.

Such distractions from their original purpose notwithstanding, the forty thousand soldiers who assembled at Constantinople in May 1097 were as fine a force as western Europe could muster. Alexius was understandably nervous, given his experience with Peter and Walter, about having such a massive force on his doorstep. He demanded that the leading crusaders take an oath of loyalty, swearing that any lands they recovered from the Turks would be turned over to Byzantium. Dependent on the Byzantine emperor for provisions, most of the nobles leading the crusade reluctantly agreed.

Finally, before open warfare broke out, Alexius agreed to send a Byzantine army to accompany the crusaders across the Bosporus and toward Palestine. The first major Turkish city they encountered was Nicaea. After a short siege, the Turkish commander agreed in secret to surrender, but only to the Byzantines. Thus it was that the crusaders awoke one morning to find Byzantine flags flying over Nicaea. Furthermore, the Westerners were forbidden to loot the city, and this act of Greek "treachery" sowed further discord.

Ultimately, the First Crusade, which lasted another two years, succeeded in wresting Palestine and Jerusalem from the Turks. It would prove to be, in fact, the only crusade that actually achieved its military objective.

Crusaders engage in battle with Turks during the First Crusade. The crusaders successfully, though briefly, took Palestine from the Turks.

Slaughter of the Jews

One of most inglorious aspects of the Crusades was the attacks on Jews by crusaders as they passed through central Europe. Twelfth-century historian Albert of Aix gave this account of the actions of Christian troops in the German city of Mainz:

The Jews of this city . . . fled in hope of safety to Bishop Rothard [who] placed the Jews in the very spacious hall of his own house . . . that they might remain safe and sound in a very secure and strong place. But Emico [a German count] and the rest of his band held a council and, after sunrise, attacked the Jews in the hall with arrows and lances. Breaking the bolts and doors, they killed the Jews, about seven hundred in number, who in vain resisted the force and attack of so many thousands. They killed the women, also, and with their swords pierced tender children of whatever age and sex. The Jews, seeing that their Christian enemies were attacking them and their children, and that they were sparing no age, likewise fell upon one another, brother, children, wives, and sisters, and thus they perished at each other's hands. Horrible to say, mothers cut the throats of nursing children with knives and stabbed others, preferring them to perish thus by their own hands rather than to be killed by the weapons of the uncircumcised.

Quoted in *Emico and the Slaughter of the Rhineland Jews*, in *Internet Medieval Sourcebook*, Paul Halsall, editor. www.fordham.edu/halsall/source/1096jews.html.

In doing so, however, the First Crusade only lay the groundwork for future conflict between the West and Byzantium. The crusaders ignored their oath to Alexius. Instead of yielding to him the areas they conquered, they established their own kingdoms—Jerusalem, Antioch, Edessa, and Tripoli—known collectively in Western Europe as Outremer, French for "beyond the sea." Instead of helping Byzantium recover the territory it had lost to the Muslims, the crusaders set up their own rival states that not only threatened Byzantine power but cut deeply into Byzantine trade.

The Byzantines could derive some comfort from the First Crusade, however. The crusader kingdoms could be counted on to relieve the Turks' pressure on Constantinople. But when the fortunes of warfare tipped in the Turks' favor, that turn of events unleashed another flood of warriors from the West—the Second Crusade.

The Second Crusade

The event that triggered the Second Crusade was the conquest of Edessa by the great Turkish general Zangi in 1144.

This crusader kingdom had long been the most vulnerable, established by Geoffrey of Bouillon between the headwaters of the Tigris and Euphrates rivers and surrounded on three sides by hostile Turks. Its fall, however, shocked Europe, and in December 1145 Pope Eugenius III called for a crusade to regain the lost territory.

The response throughout Europe was underwhelming. It was finally another emotional sermon, this one by the highly respected abbot Bernard of Clairvaux, that brought results. King Louis VII of France, who was in Bernard's audience, was so moved that he took a crusader's vow on the spot, hundreds of his knights and nobles joining him.

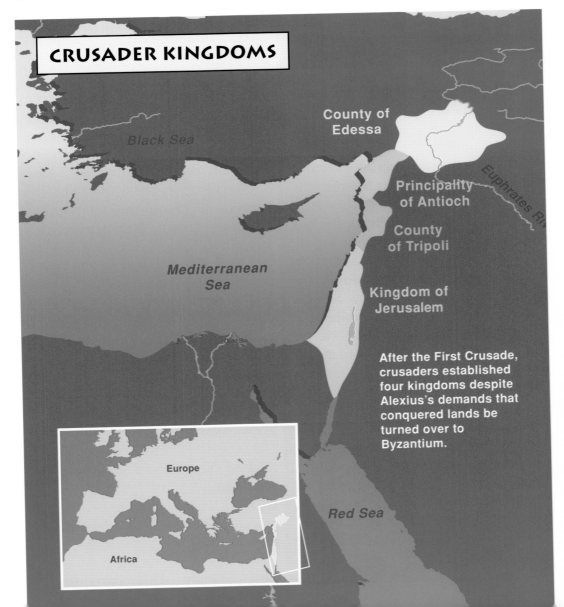

CRUSADER KINGDOMS

Black Sea

County of Edessa

Euphrates River

Principality of Antioch

County of Tripoli

Mediterranean Sea

Kingdom of Jerusalem

After the First Crusade, crusaders established four kingdoms despite Alexius's demands that conquered lands be turned over to Byzantium.

Europe

Africa

Red Sea

The other great European monarch, Conrad III of the Holy Roman Empire, a collection of German states, remained unenthusiastic, but he, too, was at last convinced by one of Bernard's sermons. Conrad's massive army, about the same size as that of Peter the Hermit but vastly superior, departed in May 1147. When Conrad reached Byzantine territory, he swore an oath that his troops would respect the people whose lands they marched through. They failed to do so, however, and sporadic fighting and looting marked the route to Constantinople.

The squabbling did not stop there, and at one point Conrad was so provoked with his host, Byzantine emperor Manuel Comnenus, that he vowed to return, once his mission was accomplished, and sack Constantinople. The two rulers patched things up, however, and Conrad crossed the Bosporus just as Louis and his forces began to arrive.

The Second Crusade was a military disaster. Conrad, not waiting for Louis, marched south and barely escaped with his life when his army was annihilated by a Turkish ambush. With only a few dozen knights, he retreated and at last joined Louis at Nicaea.

Louis fared little better. His army, too, was ambushed by the Turks, and the French king had to spend the night hidden in a tree to avoid capture. A large part of the French army escaped the Turks, however, and at length reached Jerusalem, unsure of what to do next. A force set out to attack Damascus, but retreated after only four days. Shortly afterward, both Conrad and Louis left for home. The original objective of the crusade, Edessa, had never been approached and remained in Muslim hands.

Saladin

The first two crusades left a bitter taste in the mouths of western Europeans, and it would take forty years and a major catastrophe before another could be mounted. The author of that catastrophe was Sultan Salah Ad-din, known to the crusaders as Saladin. In 1187 he launched an all-out attack on the crusader states. He won an enormous victory at Hattin, and a few months later Jerusalem surrendered to him.

The fall of Jerusalem shocked Christendom into mounting another crusade. Pope Urban III immediately sent appeals to King Henry II of England and King Philip II of France to take up the cross. They were actually at war with each other at the time, but got caught up in the emotion of the moment and agreed to join forces. Before they could set out, however, Henry died. His place was taken by his son, known to history as Richard the Lion-Hearted.

England's King Richard the Lion-Hearted leaves for the Holy Land on the Third Crusade. Richard and Turkish general Saladin ended the crusade with a truce.

Barbarossa

Getting the jump on both the English and French monarchs was a third, German emperor Frederick I, nicknamed Barbarossa because of his red beard. He had gone on the Second Crusade as a teenager and now, at almost seventy, he was eager to lead one himself. He assembled a huge army and set out in May 1188, taking the traditional overland route.

Both Saladin and the Byzantine emperor, Isaac Angelus, felt so threatened by Frederick's reputation and the size of his army that they reached a secret agreement. Isaac's troops in the Balkans would harass the crusaders with the intent of depleting them so they could not harm either the Byzantines or the Turks. Isaac's tactics, however, failed to slow the march of the Germans and only added to the ill feeling between Byzantines and crusaders. Frederick spent the winter at Edirne, about 50 miles (80km) west of Constantinople, and the two sides skirmished until the crusaders crossed into Asia the next spring.

Frederick's role in the Third Crusade ended shortly afterward when he was thrown from a horse while crossing a river and drowned. His army broke apart, many returning home and the rest joining the French and English.

The remainder of the crusade was largely the story of the maneuvering between two master generals, Richard and Saladin. After more than a year of fighting during which neither was able to gain and hold the upper hand, they signed a treaty in September 1192 that left Jerusalem under Muslim rule, but granted access to Christian pilgrims.

Despite the treaty, which had in part attained the original objective of the First Crusade, the Third Crusade was considered an embarrassing failure throughout Europe. It would not be long before another venture was begun. The first three crusades, while they had vastly increased the tension between West and East, had proved only a minor irritant to Byzantium. The fourth, however, would be a disaster.

Chapter Two

CALL TO ARMS

The failure of the Third Crusade was considered a calamity by most of western Europe. The newly installed pope, Innocent III, however, saw in yet another crusade a series of opportunities—to halt warfare between Christian kings, to win back the Holy Land, and to establish the supremacy of the papacy. He could scarcely have known that his grand plan would divide Christendom as never before.

Innocent proclaimed a new crusade in a letter issued on June 15, 1198. His zeal and emotion echoed that of Urban II a century earlier. "Jerusalem has been unhappily wasted and its Christian population slaughtered," he wrote. "Wherefore we are stricken with anguish and weeping over so great a disaster. . . . Let us collectively and individually prepare ourselves by next March 1199 to defend the land where our Lord was born."[4]

The pope's ringing call to arms was largely ignored by Europe's kings. Past crusades had required huge investments and had produced little positive outcome. Besides, the monarchs were too busy fighting one another to consider joining forces. Two princes were battling for control of the Holy Roman Empire, and Richard of England and Philip II of France were at war again. Innocent's target date for the start of the new crusade came and went with no results.

Fulk of Neuilly

It was an itinerant preacher, Fulk of Neuilly, who at last managed to kindle enthusiasm for the venture. He traversed northern France, his fiery sermons drawing thousands of listeners. A contemporary chronicler, Ralph of Coggeshall, wrote that "they hastened in large numbers: rich and poor, nobles and the base [commoners] alike, the old along with the young, an innumerable multitude of both sexes. And they eagerly received the sign of the Cross from him."[5]

The crusade, however, needed leaders —men of high standing—in addition to a multitude. Since it appeared the kings would be of no help, Innocent appealed to Europe's prominent nobles. His call was answered in November 1199 during a gathering of the flower of French chivalry at a tournament at the town of Écry near Reims. Here, amid much pomp and pageantry, Count Thibaut of Champagne and Count Louis of Blois took solemn vows to go on the crusade.

Both men were of the highest nobility —grandsons of King Louis VII of France and nephews of both Philip II and Richard—and ruled over some of the wealthiest lands in France. With Thibaut and Louis as their examples, other luminaries began to come forth, including the equally powerful Count Baldwin of Flanders.

Tournament of Écry

One of the most enthusiastic responses to Pope Innocent III's call for a crusade occurred at a great tournament at Écry near the French city of Reims. At this point of the Middle Ages, tournaments were not the stylized pageants usually depicted in modern media, writes historian Jonathan Phillips, but "far more chaotic and considerably more brutal."

Instead of a well-defined jousting course in front of a grandstand, tournaments in the eleventh century were conducted over an entire landscape. The tournament at Écry covered the entire distance between Écry and the nearby village of Balham 2.5 miles (4km) away.

Such space was needed because the mounted knights, rather than engaging in single combat, formed opposing contingents numbering as many as two hundred apiece. When a signal was given, the two sides came together in a discordant crash of shouting men, neighing horses, and clashing swords.

Injuries were common and expected. No one was supposed to be killed, at least intentionally, but sometimes suppressed rivalries erupted with deadly consequences. It was all considered great sport and preparation for real warfare. Phillips quotes the twelfth-century English knight Roger of Howden as claiming that "he is not fit for battle who has never seen his own blood flow, who has not heard his teeth crush under the blow of an opponent, or felt the full weight of his adversary upon him."

Jonathan Phillips, *The Fourth Crusade and the Sack of Constantinople*. New York: Viking, 2004, pp. 41–42.

Meanwhile another preacher, Abbot Martin of Pairis, a town in the Alsace region of Germany, was having some success. Speaking to a huge crowd at the cathedral in Basel, in modern-day Switzerland, he urged his listeners in emotionally charged language to "hasten to help Christ. Enlist in his Christian army. Rush to join the happy ranks." Finally, as if to underscore the urgency, he vowed to take the cross himself "and share in all your successes and trials."[6] Thousands surged forward to join him.

Making Plans

By the spring of 1200 enough nobles and their retinues had joined the crusade that the leaders gathered in the French city of Soissons to start some serious planning. The first crucial question was transportation. They rejected the traditional overland route. One reason was the increasing hostility between the Byzantines and Europeans as a result of the first three crusades. Another was that the Turks controlled far more of the territory along the route than before. So, despite the distaste of landsmen for sea voyages, they decided that the sea route was the quickest and easiest way.

Of the participating states, Flanders alone had a fleet, but it was far too small. The only western powers who could transport a massive army across the Mediterranean were the Italian states of Genoa, Pisa, and Venice. Genoa and Pisa, both on the western side of the

Italian peninsula, were fierce rivals and neither was willing to divert its resources toward the East.

That left Venice, and it was there in February 1201 that the crusaders sent six representatives—two each appointed by the counts of Champagne, Blois, and Flanders. The leaders of the crusade placed complete trust in their six envoys, giving them blank sheets of parchment bearing the seals of the three counts. By doing so, they were vowing to stand behind any agreement that was reached with Venice and recorded on the parchment.

Venice

Venice was the richest city in western Europe. Thanks to its location on small islands in a marshy lagoon, it had largely escaped the ravages of barbarian invasions in earlier centuries. When the Roman Empire split into East and West, Venice remained in the eastern sphere and for many years was the westernmost outpost of Byzantium. Venice became independent in the 800s and was ruled by the merchant class headed by a popularly elected leader called the doge.

The doge of Venice in 1201 was a remarkable man who was to play a pivotal part in the Fourth Crusade. Enrico Dandolo, blind and in his mid-eighties, had been elected in 1192. Venice had prospered greatly under his rule, expanding trade and defeating the Pisans in war. Despite his physical limitations, Dandolo was a man of vast experience

The seafaring merchants of medieval Venice made their city the richest in all Europe. The city played a major role in the Fourth Crusade.

and a strong ruler passionately dedicated to the welfare of Venice.

Thanks to Venice having once been part of the Byzantine Empire, the city had historically enjoyed close ties with Constantinople. Recently, however, that relationship had become strained. Venetian merchants had been expelled from Constantinople in 1171, and, although their rights were later restored under a treaty Dandolo negotiated in 1199, their historic position of favor had been undercut by the Pisans and Genoese.

Dandolo greeted the crusaders' ambassadors with great ceremony. He asked what they wanted—although he probably already knew, through his representatives in France, what was afoot. The six

envoys requested a meeting with the doge and his council, which was set for four days later. One of the envoys, Geoffrey of Villehardouin, later wrote in his account of the crusade that at this meeting the crusaders said, "Because [the French counts] know that no people have such great power to help them as you and your people; therefore we pray you by God that you take pity on the land overseas and the shame of Christ and use diligence [take care] that our lords have ships for transport and battle."[7]

The Decision

Dandolo replied that he and his council would need eight days to consider the matter and reach a decision. When the time had passed, the crusaders returned to the palace to hear what Dandolo had to offer. Venice, he said, would furnish enough ships to carry forty-five hundred knights and their horses, nine thousand squires, and twenty thousand foot soldiers. Included would be enough provisions for both men and horses for a year. The fee was to be four marks, equivalent to about $240, for each horse and two marks for each man. Ville-hardouin did not mention having given the doge an estimate of the size of the army, but the Venetians could hardly have been expected to name a price without some idea.

Altogether, then, the Venetians would be paid eighty-five thousand marks—an enormous sum for that time, about equal to twice the annual income of the king of France. The Venetians had more to offer than just passage, however. "For the love of God," said Dandolo, "we will add to the fleet fifty armed galleys on condition that, so long as we act in company, of all conquests in land or money, whether at sea or on dry ground, we shall have the half, and you the other half."[8]

Venice's Opportunities

The doge and his council, then, clearly had seen in the crusade an opportunity to enrich their city with money, land, and prestige. Some historians have called the Venetians greedy and accused them of distorting the noble purpose of a crusade. Indeed, the rewards for Venice stood to be great, but so, too, were the risks. The venture meant that the Venetians would have to build many ships in addition to the ones already available. Committing their fleet to the crusade meant that the entire maritime commerce of the city would cease for more than a year. Moreover, not only the wealth of the city but the lives of many of its sailors and soldiers would be at stake.

Still, the purpose of the crusade was supposed to be the liberation of the Holy Land, not booty for the crusaders. The

Enrico Dandolo was the leader, or doge, of Venice at the time of the Fourth Crusade and a major player in its tragic tale.

agreement was not at all what Pope Innocent had envisioned, and he approved it with some reluctance. But by this time events had moved beyond his control and he had little choice. If he wanted the crusade to go forward, it had to be under the terms of the contract.

Indeed, the crusade had evolved so that in some ways it differed significantly from what Innocent had envisioned. For one thing, the initial target of the crusade would be Egypt, not Palestine. Militarily, this was sound strategy, even though it meant more fighting. The failure of the Second and Third Crusades and the subsequent success of the Turks had left only a slim stretch of the Mediterranean coastline in Christian hands. The seat of Turkish power was in Egypt with its great cities of Alexandria and Cairo. A successful invasion of Egypt, therefore, would give the crusaders a much stronger base from which they could move north toward Jerusalem. In addition, a strong Christian presence in Egypt would help guarantee Jerusalem's future safety from the Turks.

Pope Innocent III invoked a Fourth Crusade, hoping to reunite the Eastern and Western churches, but the crusade had the opposite result.

The Size of the Army

The entire direction and outcome of the Fourth Crusade derived from a single miscalculation—the estimate of the number of troops that could be raised. Historians have long debated how and why Geoffrey of Villehardouin and his fellow envoys promised a force of 33,500 men.

Some historians have accused the French envoys of being naive and having unrealistic expectations. Others, without much in the way of evidence, have accused the Venetian doge, Dandolo, of helping to inflate the number so as to increase the amount to be paid to his city.

The envoys, however, were experienced soldiers who had some precedents to follow in calculating how many troops would be needed for the crusade. A Nor-man campaign to Egypt in 1187, in which Venice had helped transport soldiers, had numbered fifty thousand. The successful siege of Acre during the Third Crusade had required thirty-five thousand.

Historian Michael Angold writes that the envoys had some reasons to be confident in their estimate. First, the bulk of the force, twenty thousand men, would be foot soldiers instead of knights and presumably be recruited from among ordinary pilgrims. Second, the envoys had seen the success of Fulk of Neuilly's preaching and thought it would continue. Even so, writes Angold, "4,500 knights represented a very large force."

Michael Angold, *The Fourth Crusade.* Harlow, UK: Longman, 2003, p. 81.

A Secret Strategy

Sound strategy or not, the intention to attack Egypt was kept a secret. According to Villehardouin, "It was notified to the council that we should go to Babylon [as he called Cairo] . . . but to the folk at large it was only told that we were bound to go overseas."[9]

There were at least three reasons for the deception. First, of course, the truth would have put the Turks in Egypt on guard. Second, given the division of spoils in the treaty with the Venetians, it would have seemed like a grab for riches rather than for military advantage. Third, the common soldiers and many of the lesser knights were devoted to the goal of freeing Jerusalem. They might have been less willing to set sail had they known their destination was not the Holy Land.

Dandolo evidently had some doubts also, not only that the Venetian people would accept an invasion of Egypt, but also that they would approve of the venture in the first place. When the Western envoys informed the doge they would accept the terms he proposed, he said that before the contract could be signed he would have to gain the assent of his people. He was extraordinarily careful in bringing about such agreement.

Dandolo had heretofore consulted only the Small Council, a group of his closest advisers. He now took the terms of the treaty to the Grand Council, which was composed of forty leading citizens. Some of these men must have had misgivings, because Villehardouin wrote that Dandolo, by "his wit and wisdom . . . brought them to agreement and approval."[10]

The doge then consulted various other Venetians and, when he had obtained general agreement, took the final step of putting the plan before the common people. While he may have held out the promise of wealth in persuading his councilors to approve the crusade, his appeal to the general population was calculated to elicit an emotional response. He called for a special mass to be said in St. Mark's Cathedral, and—according to Villehardouin—ten thousand people attended.

"We Consent!"

After the mass, Dandolo asked his people —many of whom doubtless already knew at least something about what had been proposed—to "pray to God for counsel on the request and messages that had been addressed to them."[11] The six envoys then entered the church, walking down the central aisle to the steps leading up to the altar. They told the throng that they had been sent by the barons of France, who begged Venice to help in this holy undertaking. After this speech, Villehardouin wrote, the envoys fell weeping to their knees in supplication, whereupon the doge and all the people "burst into tears of pity and compassion, and cried with one voice, and lifted up their hands, saying, 'We consent! We consent.' Then was there so great a noise and tumult that it seemed as if the earth itself were falling to pieces."[12]

The next day the treaty was drawn up, and yet another emotional scene took place. When the seals of Venice had been added to those of the three French counts, Dandolo brought the treaty to the envoys. Overcome by the enormous task that lay ahead, he knelt weeping and, placing his hand on some holy relics, vowed to uphold the terms agreed on. The members of his council likewise took an oath, as did the envoys, while "many a tear was there shed."[13]

Then it was time for more practical matters. The first of four installment payments was not due to Venice until August, but the envoys were eager to get things under way. They borrowed five thousand marks from Venetian merchants so that shipbuilding could begin. It was agreed that the fleet would be

A painting depicts the intense emotions felt in St. Mark's Cathedral as Venetians and French nobles swear an oath to work together to retake the Holy Land.

ready for the crusading army that was to gather at Venice in May 1202.

Some Doubts

The six Frenchmen then began their long journey home. Their mission had been successful, but it would not be surprising if they harbored doubts. They had based their estimates of the size of the crusading army not only on which nobles had promised to participate, but also on who else they thought might still be persuaded to take the cross. Since each participant was supposed to pay his own way, it was essential to the success of the entire venture that the army reach the size expected by the Venetians. Otherwise, the crusaders would fall short of the agreed-upon sum for passage.

Even if the army that was raised met expectations, there was additional cause for concern. Nobles other than those who had dispatched the envoys to Venice were not bound by the contract. Even if they agreed to join the crusade, they were free to travel from whatever port or by whatever route they wished.

The six envoys were experienced men and had probably estimated the size of their army after much careful deliberation. If Villehardouin was aware of the flaws inherent in the treaty, he did not say so. These flaws, however, were to prove fatal, for they were the hinges on which the entire crusade would swing away from its intended target.

Chapter Three

DIVERSIONS

The French envoys had scarcely left Venice when their carefully laid plans began to unravel. By the time the crusaders finally assembled—much later and far fewer than anticipated—they were unable to meet the terms of their contract with the Venetians. Consequently, the only way the Fourth Crusade could proceed was in an entirely different direction than Pope Innocent envisioned.

Geoffrey of Villehardouin was barely out of Italy when he encountered another noble of Champagne, Walter of Brienne, at the head of a large body of troops. Instead of crusading, however, they were headed to recover some land belonging to Walter's wife, Elvira. Although Walter promised to join the crusade, Villehardouin wrote, "Events fall out as God wills, and never had they the power to join the host."[14] It was an episode that would be often repeated elsewhere.

There was more bad news when Villehardouin reached Champagne. Count Thibaut, only twenty-two years old, lay seriously ill. He revived somewhat on hearing the news from Venice and even rose from his bed to go riding. The exertion, however, proved too much, and he died a few days afterward.

The loss of Thibaut was a serious blow to the crusade. Just by the force of his personality, the charismatic young count had drawn many knights to take the cross. With his death, some of those he had attracted began to drift away. In addition, he left an infant son as count, a situation that doubtless left some of his vassals inclined to stay home and guard their estates from neighbors looking to take advantage of the situation.

Boniface

Then, too, there was the question of who would lead the crusade. Thibaut had shared command equally with the counts of Blois and Flanders, but his death seems to have left such a void that a supreme commander, someone to supersede the two counts, was thought necessary. Finally, at another meeting at Soissons, Villehardouin, according to his own account, proposed that command be offered to Boniface, marquis of Montferrat.

In many ways Boniface was an excellent choice. An accomplished soldier, he knew the East well. His father had fought in the Second Crusade and two older brothers were veterans of the Third Crusade. He was wealthy and powerful, his territory encompassing some of the richest land in northern Italy. His court was famous throughout Europe, in the words of one of his knights,

Christian nobles charge into battle during the failed Second Crusade. Boniface of Montferrat was chosen to lead the Fourth Crusade because his father had fought in the second and his brothers in the third.

Raimbaut of Vaquerias, as a place of "munificence and services of ladies, elegant raiment [dress], handsome armor, trumpets and diversions."[15] Such a man could be expected to attract many recruits to the crusade.

Accordingly, envoys were sent to Boniface, who agreed to come to Soissons. After a glittering reception, he met with the leading crusaders in an orchard to hear their offer, which included not only command of the crusade, but also a large sum of money left for the cause by Thibaut. Boniface accepted in yet another emotional scene, all parties kneeling and weeping, then was led into a nearby church, where a cross was attached to his shoulder.

Prince Alexius

Before returning to Montferrat, Boniface paid a visit to his good friend Prince Philip of Swabia, one of the contenders for rule of the Holy Roman Empire. While at Philip's court he met Philip's brother-in-law, Prince Alexius of Constantinople. Alexius's father, Byzantine emperor Isaac II, had been overthrown by his brother, who became Emperor Alexius III. The deposed emperor had been blinded and thrown into prison along with his son. The younger Alexius managed to escape in 1201 and made his way to Germany to enlist Philip's help to restore his father as emperor. It was there that he met Boniface.

There is no record of their conversations, but it would have been strange if Alexius had not included Boniface in his appeal for help. Neither Boniface nor Philip, however, was in a position to come to Alexius's aid. The prince then traveled to Rome to seek help from Pope Innocent, but the pope had recently exchanged letters with Emperor Alexius and was hoping for a thaw in relations between the eastern and western branches of Christianity. Innocent, therefore, was disinclined to back the prince.

Contract in Trouble

Meanwhile, the timetable established by the contract with Venice was in jeopardy. Boniface, for instance, arrived back in Montferrat about May 1202—nine months after he had departed and only a month before the crusaders were supposed to sail. He wrote to the French counts, telling them he would join them when he could.

Similar delays occurred throughout Europe as crusaders tried to raise the money necessary for the venture, gather weapons and supplies, and generally put their affairs in order. Everything seemed to take longer than expected, and many knights did not even set out for Venice—a journey of about six weeks from northern France—until the projected sailing date had passed. The problem was that the army, like all armies of the Crusades, was not an organized, disciplined force, but, as historians Donald Queller and Thomas Madden write, "an inchoate [formless]

A nineteenth-century painting depicts marching crusaders. Participants in the Fourth Crusade met frustrating delays and diversions throughout the campaign.

mass of men moved unpredictably by enthusiasms, fears, ambitions, superstitions, and lusts."[16]

Move, however, the crusaders finally did—in small groups and large over several months. There were the usual tearful goodbyes as warriors left their families, not knowing when—or if—they would see them again. Robert of Clari, a Frenchman who wrote an account of the Fourth Crusade from an ordinary knight's viewpoint, noted, "Many there were of fathers and moth-ers, wives and children, who made great lamenting over their loved ones."[17]

Arriving in Venice

Throughout the summer of 1202 the crusaders straggled into Venice. There was not enough room for them inside the city proper, so they camped on the island of St. Nicholas. Those who arrived early—actually at the date agreed on—endured long weeks of boredom. As might have been expected, tempers grew short and fights occurred frequently between men who came from regions that were traditional rivals.

By the time Boniface and his men arrived on August 15, it was clear that the six envoys had greatly overestimated the size of the army. Nowhere near the number of men promised to the Venetians were on hand. The contract called for payment of passage for 33,500 troops. Fewer than half, an estimated 12,000, had shown up. Villehardouin, perhaps seeking to avoid taking a share of the blame for overestimating the numbers, . . . harshly criticized those crusaders who chose alternate routes. "Ah! The grievous harm and loss when those who should have come thither sailed instead from other ports,"[18] he wrote, ignoring the fact that they were free to do so.

Some crusaders thought the Venetians should transport them at the agreed-on price per man, even though the contract called for full payment based on a much larger army and a fleet had been prepared for the full number. The crusade's leaders, however, asked their respective nobles to make up the difference. Much was collected, wrote Villehardouin, "many a fine vessel of gold and silver [but] there was still wanting . . . 34,000 marks of silver."[19]

A New Plan

The French and their allies were in a bad spot, but so were the Venetians. They not only faced a huge financial loss, but also had a potentially hostile army on their doorstep. Dandolo, however, had a plan, one far from fulfilling the original purpose of the crusade. Venice would postpone demanding the remainder of the payment if the crusaders would help recover the city of Zara, which lay about 165 miles (266km) from Venice on the eastern coast of the Adriatic Sea. Long under the control of Venice, Zara had broken away some twenty years earlier and was now under the protection of Enrico, king of Hungary.

Dandolo announced the plan at a service in the cathedral. In a speech that indicates that he was not solely motivated by power or gain, he said, "I am an old man and feeble, who should have need of rest [but] if you will consent that I take the sign of the cross . . . then shall I go to live or die with you, and with the pilgrims [crusaders]."[20]

The Venetians reacted joyously, but the offer caused an uproar among the leading crusaders. For one thing, Zara was a Christian city loyal to the pope. For another, Enrico, although he had yet to appear in Venice, had agreed to participate in the crusade. Pope Innocent, likewise, could not condone the plan. He wrote a letter to the crusaders saying that any who attacked Zara would be excommunicated. Before the letter arrived, however, the fleet had already sailed.

The crusaders had had little choice but to accept Dandolo's offer. If they refused, their only recourse was to return home in humiliation or find some other route to Egypt. Even so, some crusaders departed for home rather than take this

Unable to Pay

When the soldiers of the Fourth Crusade gathered in Venice, there were not enough of them to pay the negotiated passage money to the Venetians. The reaction of Dandolo, doge of Venice, was recorded by Robert of Clari:

When the doge and the Venetians saw that the pilgrims [crusaders] had not paid them more than this [an amount short of the total called for], they were all very angry. Finally, the doge said to them: "Lords," said he, "you have used us ill, for as soon as your messengers had made the bargain with me I commanded through all my land that no trader should go a-trading, but that all should help prepare this navy. So they have waited ever since and have not made any money for a year and a half past. Instead, they have lost a great deal, and therefore we wish, my men and I, that you should pay us the money you owe us. And if you do not do so, then know that you shall not depart from this island [of Saint Nicholas, where the crusaders were quartered] before we are paid, nor shall you find anyone to bring you anything to eat or drink." [But] the doge was a right worthy man, and so he did not cease from having brought to them enough to eat and to drink.

Robert of Clari, *The Conquest of Constantinople.* Translated by Edgar Holmes McNeal. New York: W.W. Norton, 1936, p. 40.

new course. Even Boniface would arrange to be absent, saying he would rejoin the army after tending to urgent matters in Montferrat.

The Fleet Sails

The number of ships that left Venice in October 1202 has generally been estimated at about two hundred. About half would have been needed for horses, with one fourth to transport troops and the rest consisting of galleys outfitted as warships. From all accounts, the departing fleet was a magnificent sight. Dandolo's galley was painted a bright red, and the doge sat on a throne underneath a canopy of red silk. Drums pounded and silver trumpets blared. Clari wrote that "it was the finest thing to see that has ever been since the beginning of the world."[21]

After a pause at the port of Pola, the fleet arrived before Zara on November 10. It was a formidable city—"Vainly would you have sought for a fairer city, or one of greater strength, or richer,"[22] wrote Villehardouin—yet its citizens knew they were no match for the army facing them. When the city leaders offered to surrender, however, the deep divisions among the crusaders came to the surface.

Even as Dandolo and the leading crusaders were conferring about the offer of surrender, those who had opposed the mission to Zara, led by Simon of Montfort, went to the city's envoys and told them, wrote Villehardouin, that the Venetians, not the crusaders, were their enemies. "The pilgrims will not attack you," he said. "Have no care of them. If you can defend yourself against the Venetians, all will be well."[23] In addition, the pope's letter forbidding the attack on Zara and threatening excommunication to anyone who disobeyed had caught up with the crusade. A French abbot, Guy of Vaux, produced a copy of the letter from Pope Innocent. He read it to the crusaders, hoping they would then force the Venetians to abandon the attack on Zara and resume the crusade.

Dandolo was furious. According to Clari, he vowed, "I will not in any degree give over [yield] . . . not even for the apostolic see [the pope]."[24] The crusade's leaders had a difficult choice—attack the city and face the pope's wrath or obey the pope and risk abandonment by the Venetians and the end of the crusade. They decided to side with the Venetians, but in order to keep their troops complacent, they suppressed the news of the pope's threat.

Siege of Zara

The siege of Zara began on November 13. The city resisted every attack, but when the crusaders began to tunnel beneath the city walls, intending to set fires that would weaken the walls from below and bring them down, the city surrendered, the only condition being that the inhabitants' lives would be spared. On November 24, the gates were opened and the victors stormed in. They seized almost everything of value, even plundering churches.

By now, winter had arrived, and because of the danger posed by storms there was no way for the army to sail farther. Boredom set in, tempers grew short, and there was one serious conflict between the French and Venetians in which about one hundred men were killed. After peace was restored, the crusaders settled down to wait for spring and—they thought— the voyage to Egypt. But another diversion, this one rooted in the dispute over the Byzantine throne, was about to arise.

Shortly after Boniface returned from Montferrat and rejoined the army in mid-December, envoys arrived representing Philip of Swabia and Prince Alexius. They proposed that the crusade proceed not to Egypt, but to Constantinople to restore Alexius's father, Isaac, to the throne. In return, Alexius promised to place the Eastern church under the authority of the pope and to pay the crusaders 200,000 silver marks, or about $12 million. He also promised to accompany them to Egypt once his father had regained his throne and to bring ten thousand troops with him.

The proposal clearly offered something to all sides. The pope would be able

Departure of the Fleet

When at last the crusading fleet departed from Venice in October 1202, it must have been a magnificent sight, especially to ordinary knights and soldiers from France who had never seen a force so large or even been to sea. One such knight, Robert of Clari, described the departure this way:

Then they all got ready their gear and their navy and put to sea. And each of the high men had his own ship for himself and his people, and his transport to carry his horses, and the doge [of Venice] had with him fifty galleys all at his own cost. The galley he was in was all vermilion and it had a canopy of vermilion samite [a heavy silk] spread over him, and there were four silver trumpets trumpeting before him and drums making a great noise. And all the high men, and the clerks [clergy] and laymen, and great and small, displayed so much joy at the departure that never yet was there such rejoicing, nor was ever such a fleet seen or heard of. And the pilgrims [crusaders] had all the priests and clerks mount on the high poops [decks] of the ships to chant the *Veni creator spiritus* ["Come, creator spirit"]. And everyone, great and small, wept with emotion and for the great joy they had.

Robert of Clari, *The Conquest of Constantinople*. Translated by Edgar Holmes McNeal. New York: W.W. Norton, 1936, p. 42.

---

to reunite both branches of Christianity under his control. The Venetians would get the balance of the money owed to them in addition to what they had reaped from the sack of Zara. The crusaders would be able to pay their debt with a tidy sum left over, continue the crusade after the detour to Constantinople, and be back in the pope's good graces.

The offer intrigued the crusade's leaders, but most of their men were unenthusiastic. In fact, many more than before joined Simon of Montfort and Abbot Guy in protesting. "Then arose much debate," Villehardouin wrote in a decided understatement. "There was discord in the host."[25] According to Clari, those opposing the offer said, "Bah! What shall we be doing in Constantinople? We have our pilgrimage [the crusade] to make, and also our plan for going to [Cairo] or Alexandria. Moreover, our [Venetian] navy is to follow us for only a year, and half of the year is already past."[26]

Those who favored the plan countered that, even so, the French owed the

Doge Dandolo leads the siege of the city of Zara. Zara's fall brought fortune to the Venetians but little benefit to the crusaders.

Venetians a large sum and would have no way to continue the crusade without accepting Alexius's offer. They would have to return home in disgrace and, thanks to their attack on Zara, possibly under excommunication.

The debate raged on, but Dandolo, Boniface, Count Baldwin, and Count Louis were determined to accept Alexius's offer, reasoning that only with the men and money the prince promised could they continue the crusade. They summoned his envoys, drew up the agreement, and asked their nobles to take an oath to uphold it. There was little enthusiasm, even among the nobles. Villehardouin admits, "Only twelve persons took the oaths on the side of the Franks [French], for more of sufficient note could not be found."[27]

Desertions

So deep was the division among the leading crusaders that when word of the agreement spread, some attempted to

This manuscript illumination depicts Count Baldwin of Flanders receiving a subject. Baldwin served as the first western European emperor of Constantinople after the city's fall.

Disagreement at Zara

When the crusaders arrived at Zara, intending to recapture it for the Venetians, Abbot Guy of Vaux produced a letter from Pope Innocent III forbidding the attack on a Christian city. The exchange among the abbot, the doge of Venice, and the French counts was recorded by Geoffrey of Villehardouin:

Then rose the abbot of Vaux, of the order of the Cistercians, and said to them: "Lords, I forbid you, on the part of the Pope of Rome, to attack this city; for those within it are Christians, and you are pilgrims."

When the Doge heard this, he was very wroth [angry], and much disturbed, and he said to the counts and barons: "Signors, I had this city, by their own agreement, at my mercy, and your people have broken that agreement; you have covenanted to help me to conquer it, and I summon you to do so."

Whereon the counts and barons all spoke at once, together with those who were of their party, and said: "Great is the outrage of those who have caused this agreement to be broken, and never a day has passed that they have not tried to break up the host. Now are we shamed if we do not help to take the city." And they came to the Doge, and said: "Sire, we will help you to take the city in despite of those who would let and hinder us."

Thus was the decision taken.

Geoffrey of Villehardouin, *Chronicle of the Fourth Crusade and the Conquest of Constantinople*, in *Internet Medieval Sourcebook*, Paul Halsall, editor. www.fordham.edu/halsall/basis/villehardouin.html.

---

reach the Holy Land on their own. Five hundred men commandeered a ship and were drowned when it sank. Others headed overland but were forced to turn back when they were attacked as they entered Slovenia because the residents feared the crusaders would ransack the country. Simon of Montfort and his men, including Abbot Guy, likewise departed. "Thus did the host go greatly dwindling day by day,"[28] Villehardouin wrote.

Pope Innocent, meanwhile, had received emissaries from the French crusaders begging his forgiveness for the attack on Zara. He forgave the French, saying they had acted out of necessity, but not the Venetians, whom he blamed for what he considered the perversion of the crusade. The pope wrote to the French, reluctantly allowing them to proceed on the crusade with the Venetians, but he expressly forbade them to attack Constantinople. Even though Prince Alexius's offer held out the possibility of a united Christendom, Innocent was still hopeful that such unity could be achieved by peaceful means. The pope's letter, like the earlier one threatening excommunication if Zara were attacked, was suppressed by the crusade's leaders when it arrived.

The fleet left Zara in stages throughout the spring of 1203, intending to reassemble at the island of Corfu off the western coast of Greece. Prince Alexius arrived in Zara in mid-April—without his ten thousand men—but was given a royal welcome by Dandolo and Boniface nonetheless.

After a month at Corfu, all was ready. The fleet sailed on May 24 and, according to Villehardouin, "the hearts of men rejoiced greatly."[29] After an easy voyage, the fleet left the Mediterranean, sailing through the strait of the Dardanelles and the Sea of Marmara and into the Bosporus. On the afternoon of June 23,

the crusaders dropped anchor. In the distance, about 5 miles (8km) to the northwest, they could see the towers that marked the destination most of them had never dreamed of—Constantinople.

Historians have long speculated that the diversion of the Fourth Crusade to Constantinople was a conspiracy. Some suggest that Boniface, Philip of Swabia, and Prince Alexius planned the diversion from the first and later enlisted Dandolo's help. Others claim that Dandolo was the primary culprit, making a secret agreement with the sultan of Egypt to take the crusaders elsewhere. Historians throughout the centuries have tried, and failed, to find evidence of such plots. In the absence of such evidence, what is unquestionable is that what befell Constantinople must be considered a tragedy of unprecedented proportions.

# Chapter Four

THE CITY CONQUERED

The immediate objective of the Fourth Crusade—against the expressed wishes of the pope and of many of its participants—had been diverted from Egypt to Constantinople. Its purpose, instead of retaking Jerusalem from the Muslims, was to impose a ruler on a Christian realm. Doing so proved easy—deceptively so. The French and Venetians would soon realize that their plans would require yet another change.

When they first saw Constantinople, the crusaders wondered if they had undertaken too great a task. Enclosed within its 12 miles (19km) of walls was a population estimated at 500,000—more than ten times that of Paris and London combined at that time. Those walls formed a rough triangle bounded to the west by land, to the south by the Sea of Marmara, on the eastern point of the triangle by the Bosporus, and to the

north by the narrow strait known as the Golden Horn, leading to the Black Sea. High, thick walls interspersed with towers protected the city on all sides. "No man there was of such hardihood but his flesh trembled," Villehardouin wrote, "and it was no wonder, for never was so great an enterprise undertaken by any people since the creation of the world."[30]

Constantinople, however, was not as invincible as it appeared from the outside. For one thing, it had been wracked by political turmoil. The current emperor, Alexius III, was the fourth in fifteen years, his three predecessors having been either murdered or deposed. According to Niketas Choniates, a Byzantine court official who left a detailed history of the period, the emperor "withdrew from . . . public affairs" and lived only to "supply himself with lavish luxuries and pleasures."[31]

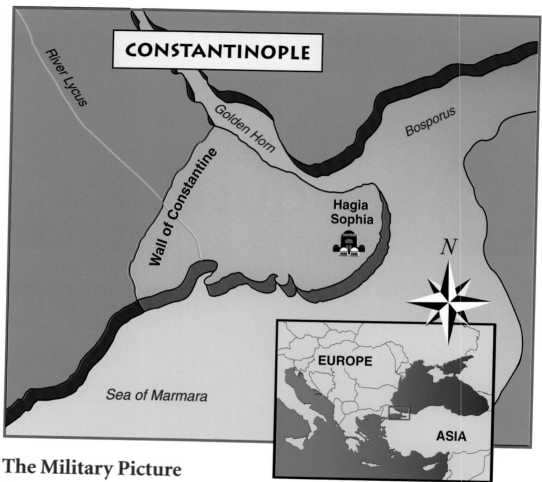

The Military Picture

The city's military situation was similarly unsound. The Byzantine emperor had come to rely increasingly on foreign mercenaries, notably his Varangian Guard, which was made up largely of Scandinavians and Anglo-Saxons. The soldiers of the Byzantine Empire itself, while numerous, were considered inferior to their foreign counterparts by Choniates, who wrote that they were chiefly interested in grants of land that were provided when they enlisted. The navy was in even worse condition, having dwindled to "rotting and worm-eaten small [ships], barely twenty in number"[32]

Still, the people of Constantinople must have felt reasonably secure on June 24 as the crusader fleet sailed past the eastern tip of the city. After all, the city, although frequently falling victim to internal revolts, had never been conquered by an outside enemy in the almost nine hundred years since its founding.

The fleet passed the city en route to landing at Scutari on the opposite side of the Bosporus. There it waited, in vain, for word that Constantinople was ready to welcome Prince Alexius and to restore his father, Isaac, to the throne. After nine days had passed, the leaders wondered if perhaps the Byzantines did not realize the prince had returned. They decided to make certain.

On July 3 ten Venetian galleys sailed slowly along the mighty walls facing the Bosporus. In one, probably Dandolo's luxurious flagship, Prince Alexius was prominently visible. Villehardouin wrote that those alongside the prince cried out, "Behold your natural lord . . . behold the rightful heir,"[33] and threatened war if he were not restored. Not a single response came from the city on

A fifteenth-century painting of the siege of Constantinople shows the Venetian fleet at the ready and the crusaders encamped before the great city.

Emperor Alexius III

Byzantine Emperor Alexius III, who deposed his brother Isaac and whose nephew Alexius the crusaders hoped to place on the throne, was held in little regard by court official Niketas Choniates. In this passage from his history, Choniates tells how, in his opinion, Alexius III let the empire decay:

Like a steersman who is compelled by the waves to let go of the rudder, he withdrew from the administration of public affairs and spent his time wearing golden ornaments and giving ear to, and granting, every petition of those who had helped raise him to power. With both hands he poured out the monies that [Isaac] had amassed, and they were scattered like heaps of chaff and blown away like summer dust. . . . Only later, when he had need of funds, did this emperor who was devoted to futile munificence censure himself for his prodigality [wastefulness]. . . . As a result of these conditions, [he] failed in all else, more so than any other emperor, and the ministries went from bad to worse. . . . [Alexius] knew no more, in fact, of what was going on in the empire than did the inhabitants of *ultima* Thule [a remote northern region, possibly Iceland].

Niketas Choniates, *O City of Byzantium: Annals of Niketas Choniates.* Translated by Harry J. Magoulias. Detroit: Wayne State University Press, 1984, pp. 252, 265.

Alexius's behalf. Indeed, the people claimed not to recognize him.

The crusaders now knew that the prince had either lied or greatly overestimated the esteem in which he was held. However, they had no choice, if they hoped to receive the 200,000 marks Alexius had promised, but to restore his father to the throne by force.

Attack on Galata

The best place for an attack on Constantinople from the sea was in the Golden Horn, where the water was much calmer than in the Bosporus or the Sea of Marmara. To reach the Golden Horn, however, the crusaders first had to capture a strong fortress opposite the city on the northern side of its entrance—the Tower of Galata—and sever the huge chain that the Byzantines stretched across the strait both to protect the city and to prevent merchant ships from entering before paying a fee.

The army landed at Galata on July 5 without opposition. That night, however, Emperor Alexius sent a raiding party across the Golden Horn by barge. It attacked the crusader camp at the same time another force charged out from the tower. The Byzantines had the advantage of surprise, but the superior skill of the crusaders soon sent the attackers retreating to the safety of the tower. Before the Byzantines had a chance to close the tower gates however, the crusaders forced the entire garrison to surrender, thus winning in a single exchange what might have taken many days to conquer otherwise.

The next day, the *Eagle*, largest of the Venetian galleys, used its ironclad keel to crash through the chain, leaving the

Crusaders scale Constantinople's great walls by using siege works while the Venetians overrun the city's battlements from their ships via flying bridges.

Golden Horn open to the invaders. What remained of the Byzantine navy was then quickly overcome, and the crusaders paused to consider their next move. They decided that each party should mount the type of attack most suited to it—the French by land and the Venetians by sea. The land assault would be directed against the Blachernae district at the northern tip of Constantinople. The fleet would strike at the less fortified walls along the northern coast.

The Attack

The French had prepared by capturing the Blachernae bridge, which spanned the Golden Horn. Then, on July 17, they divided their army into seven divisions. Three, led by Boniface, remained to guard the camp from attack while the other four, commanded by Baldwin of Flanders, advanced on the city walls with tall scaling ladders. Holding their shields above them to fend off a shower of arrows and crossbow bolts, the French reached the wall. A few succeeded in getting to the top, holding the defenders back while more of their comrades made the ascent.

Emperor Alexius, however, sent his elite Varangian Guard to repel the attack. Wielding heavy battle axes, the emperor's men slowly forced the French back down the ladders and the attack stalled.

The Venetians, meanwhile, were enjoying more success. To attack the walls,

Dandolo had ordered flying bridges to be built high in the rigging of the larger transport ships. These "marvelous engines,"[34] in Clari's words, consisted of paired wooden spars extending about 100 feet (31m) from the masts, secured with ropes and covered with planking wide enough that knights could advance three abreast. These bridges were protected by a framework covered with hides thick enough to withstand arrows. Archers posted in the rigging defended the bridges, and machines on deck hurled large stones against the walls.

Dandolo's Courage

The Venetians attacked where the city walls stood almost at the water's edge. As the skilled sailors maneuvered the large ships to a point from which the ends of the flying bridges would reach the top of the wall, the smaller galleys headed for the beach to land groups of knights and foot soldiers. One of the first arrivals was Dandolo himself, who —despite his age and blindness— threatened his crew that unless they put him ashore, he would "do justice upon their bodies with his hands."[35]

At length, knights were able to cross onto the battlements from the flying bridges. As they pushed the defenders back, others secured the bridges to the walls and troops began to pour across. The Byzantines lost their nerve and fled, allowing the Venetians to descend and open the gates from the inside. Eventually, they won control of twenty-five

Another View of Dandolo

Such eyewitness accounts of the Fourth Crusade as those by Geoffrey of Villehardouin and Robert of Clari are lavish in their praise of Dandolo, doge of Venice. The Byzantine historian Niketas Choniates, very understandably, had a different view:

The doge of Venice, Enrico Dandolo, was not the least of horrors; a man maimed in sight and along in years, a creature most treacherous and extremely jealous of the Romans [Byzantines], a sly cheat who called himself wiser than the wise and madly thirsting after glory as no other, he preferred death to allowing the Romans to escape the penalty for their insulting treatment of his nation. . . . Realizing that should he work some treachery against the Romans with his fellow countrymen, he schemed to include other accomplices, to share his secret designs with those whom he knew nursed an implacable hatred against the Romans and who looked with an envious and avaricious eye on their goods.

Niketas Choniates, *O City of Byzantium: Annals of Niketas Choniates*. Translated by Harry J. Magoulias. Detroit: Wayne State University Press, 1984, p. 295.

towers—about one-fourth of the harbor side of Constantinople.

Alarmed, Emperor Alexius sent a part of the Varangian Guard being held in reserve to expel the invaders. The Venetians had to fall back against such fierce warriors, but began to set fires to cover their escape. A strong wind whipped the blaze into the city, destroying buildings covering about 120 acres (49 hectares), displacing some twenty thousand citizens in the process. It would require, writes Choniates, "a river of tears to counterbalance the fire's extensive damage."[36]

The fire prevented the Venetians from being dislodged from the walls, so the emperor tried to draw them away. He led a large army from a gate on the western side of the city and marched north to threaten the French, hoping that the Venetians would abandon their position and rush to their allies' aid.

"The Whole World Was There Assembled"

From eyewitness accounts, the size of the Byzantine army has been estimated at thirty thousand. "When the opponent's land forces suddenly beheld this huge array, they shuddered,"[37] Choniates wrote. Villehardouin, likewise, was impressed, writing that "it seemed as if the whole world was there assembled."[38]

The French knights hastily scrambled to meet this unexpected threat. The three divisions that had been guarding the crusaders' camp joined them, and even the cooks and servants, some armed with kitchen knives and using pots and pans as helmets, were pressed into service. Three divisions led by Baldwin of Flanders, his brother Henry, and Hugh of Saint-Pol formed up facing the advancing Byzantines. The other four divisions, under Boniface, remained with the siege machines. They had strict orders to stay put unless the rest were in mortal danger.

The three divisions of crusaders, perhaps as few as four hundred mounted knights, and the Byzantines advanced slowly against each other. At one point, Baldwin wanted to withdraw, but the

In the foreground of this manuscript illumination is a trebuchet, the massive catapult used to breach fortified walls in medieval battles, including the siege of Constantinople.

others continued at a trot and Baldwin, his honor threatened, hastened to rejoin them.

Finally, both sides came to a halt, facing each other across a small river, the Lycus. The crusaders were too few in number to cross the river without losing a significant number of men in the process. The Byzantines, on the other hand, were numerous enough to cross the Lycus without seriously depleting their forces. The odds, then, greatly favored the Byzantines.

Sudden Retreat

At this point, however, the emperor seems to have lost his nerve, although historians are unsure of the reason. Perhaps Alexius feared facing the French knights on their massive warhorses in open battle. In any event, he gave the order to withdraw, leaving the French stunned at their good fortune. "Never did God save any people from such peril as He saved the host that day," Villehardouin wrote, "and be it known to you further that there was none in the host so hardy but he had great joy thereof."[39]

Emperor Alexius's people were not pleased with his evident lack of will. "He returned in utter disgrace," wrote Choniates, "having only made the enemy more haughty and insolent."[40] The emperor apparently sensed the mood of his people and, knowing the fate that had befallen many of his predecessors, decided to make the best of a bad situation. That night, taking his favorite daughter, some close associates, and 1,000 pounds (454kg) of gold, Alexius III fled from Constantinople. "It was as though he had labored hard to make a miserable corpse of the City," Choniates wrote, "to bring her to utter ruin in defiance of her destiny, and he hastened along her destruction."[41]

The next morning, court officials brought the no-doubt-astounded Isaac from his prison cell and returned him to the throne. When the news reached the crusaders there were cheers, but also caution. Would the restored emperor honor the promises made by his son? A four-man delegation, including Geoffrey of Villehardouin, was sent to find out.

The delegates entered the Blachernae Palace, walked past the glitteringly attired courtiers to the throne, and asked for a private audience, which was granted. Once closeted with Isaac, the crusaders outlined the terms of the Treaty of Zara. The emperor expressed grave doubts, especially as to the submission of the Orthodox Church to the pope. In the end, however, he agreed, probably realizing he had little choice. He also agreed to an additional demand that his son Alexius should be co-emperor.

"A Witless Lad"

The prince was crowned Alexius IV on August 1, 1203, to the disgust of Choniates, who called him "a witless lad ignorant of affairs of state."[42] He immediately began fulfilling his promises—to the extent that he was able to do so. He paid half of the contracted price—100,000 marks, or about $6 million—which was divided equally between the Venetians and the French. The French promptly paid the Venetians thirty-six thousand marks out of their share, the balance owed on the original contract.

Alexius owed the crusaders another 100,000 marks, but he did not have the money. Much of the royal treasury had been emptied by the prince's uncle before his flight. Some money was raised by imposing huge fines on those who had supported the former emperor, but it was not enough. The new co-emperor then took one of the last options open to him—melting down many of the gold and silver plates, chalices, and ornaments that adorned Constantinople's churches. While this move gained him some cash with which to pay his debt, it earned him the bitter scorn of his subjects. "In utter violation of the law, he touched the untouchable," Choniates wrote. "It was a sight to behold: the holy icons of Christ consigned to the flames after being hacked to pieces with axes and cast down . . . the revered and all-hallowed vessels seized from the churches with utter indifference and melted down and given over to the enemy troops as common silver and gold."[43]

Alexius's monetary promise was not the only one he was having trouble keeping. He wrote to Pope Innocent, seeking to justify the crusaders' disobedience of the papal commands. He asserted that the French had been drawn not chiefly by the promise of wealth, but by the chance to bring the Eastern church under Rome's dominion. However, he gave no guarantee that he would actually deliver his subjects to the pope, now saying only that he personally would work "with all his might [to] influence the Eastern Church toward the same end."[44]

In fact, Alexius must have realized that his subjects would not submit to the pope's authority. While he himself acknowledged the pope's supremacy in writing—and forced the patriarch of Constantinople to do likewise—that was as far as he went in fulfilling his original promise. When Innocent requested that the patriarch make his submission public and come to Rome to receive a sign of office from the pope, his request was ignored. In the Byzantine churches, Orthodox practices continued exactly as before.

The Money Problem

Money, however, was the principal problem, both for Alexius and the crusaders. Alexius could not pay the remainder of the debt, and the French needed that money. Although the crusaders had paid the Venetians what was owed, the contract would expire in September 1203. Unless the French came up with more cash, the Venetians were prepared to leave them stranded. Clearly a new plan was needed, and Alexius came to the crusader camp to propose one.

Alexius asked the French and Venetians to postpone once again the plans that had been made five years earlier. In

Mangonels and Trebuchets

Two of the machines of war used by the crusaders against the walls of Constantinople were mangonels and trebuchets. Both were varieties of catapults used to hurl large weights against walls or battlements.

Mangonels, from the Greek *manganon* or "war machine," were by far the earlier of the two, having been used by Greek soldiers as far back as 200 B.C. They consisted of a throwing arm inserted into a bundle of twisted ropes, the strongest of which were made from horsehair. The twisting caused such a torsion that the arm, pulled back, would spring forward at high speed. A sling attached to the arm could throw a 10-pound (4.5kg) stone more than 400 yards (366m).

Lighter versions of mangonels, small enough to be assembled on ship decks, were used in the Fourth Crusade by the Venetians. By this time, however, the heavier, land-based versions had been replaced by the trebuchet.

Instead of relying on torsion, the trebuchet, from the French *trebucher*, or "overthrow," consisted of a long arm mounted on a frame so as to pivot perpendicular to the ground. Attached to the short end of the arm was a large counterweight that, when released, would swing the longer end up in an arc, flinging stones or cannonballs from a sling. The largest trebuchets, with arms 50 feet (15m) long and counterweights of 20,000 pounds (9,080kg), could throw stones of 300 pounds (136kg) more than 300 yards (274m).

Trebuchets were highly effective against city walls, but all such engines of war would be rendered obsolete in the 1400s with the invention of gunpowder and the cannon.

the meantime, he would—with the crusaders' help—regain control of some outlying provinces that were still loyal to his uncle. Thus strengthened, he asserted, he could raise enough money to pay what he owed plus enough to finance the crusade, which would now sail in March 1204, through the following September.

Alexius also appealed to the crusaders' sense of honor. Although his own overestimation of his standing in Constantinople had led to the current quandary, he said the crusaders had an obligation to protect him. "Be it known to you, therefore, that, if you abandon me," he said candidly, "the Greeks hate me because of you: I shall lose my land, and they will kill me."[45]

Alexius's proposal, Villehardouin wrote, caused "much discord in the host, as had been oft times before."[46] The rank-and-file crusaders were furious at the prospect of another delay. The fact remained, however, that the crusade was short of both money and time. The earliest it could possibly sail would be October, which would mean it would arrive in Palestine—Egypt as an intermediary objective seems to have been forgotten—at the onset of winter, a poor time for warfare.

Once more, it seemed, the crusaders had little choice. They agreed, many very reluctantly, to Alexius's proposal. What they could not have known was that the emperor's words would be tragically prophetic and that, having conquered Constantinople once, they would be faced with the necessity of doing so again.

Chapter Five

THE CITY RECONQUERED

Achievement of the goal of the Fourth Crusade—that is, the recapture of Jerusalem—rested on whether or not the new co-emperor, Alexius IV, could keep his promises. In the end he could not, and this failure, plus tension and distrust between crusaders and Byzantines, led to conflicts that deteriorated into confrontation and finally into open warfare. The bitterness of that conflict prepared the way for the tragedy that was to befall Constantinople.

Shortly after reaching the new agreement, Alexius and Boniface set off on an expedition designed to establish the emperor's authority in areas outside Constantinople. While they were gone, the bulk of the crusaders became tourists, fascinated at the size and wealth of the city. Especially awestruck were the French, whose drafty stone castles seemed crude in comparison to the palaces of Byzantium. Robert of Clari described in

great detail the wonders he saw, summing up by writing, "All these marvels which I have recounted to you here and still a great many more than we could recount, the French found in Constantinople after they had captured it."[47]

As is so often the case, however, hostility soon grew between the conquerors and the conquered. This smoldering resentment finally burst into flame—literally—on August 19. A group of Flemings (men of Flanders) and Venetians sailed across the Golden Horn in fishing boats and, from either religious zeal, greed, or both, began to plunder a mosque. When the Muslims and their Byzantine neighbors fought back, the crusaders set the building on fire.

The Great Fire

This section of the city was densely packed with wooden houses, and the blaze spread quickly. It was soon so large, Choniates wrote, that it "proved all the [other fires] before it to be but sparks." The fire raged unchecked for two days and nights, reaching almost to the great church of Hagia Sophia in the heart of the city. Everything within an area of about 440 acres (178ha) "was consumed like candlewicks," Choniates wrote. "Woe is me! How great was the loss of those magnificent, most beautiful palaces."[48]

Fearing retaliation from the infuriated Byzantines, most Westerners living in the city took their families and possessions and moved to the crusader camp. Relations between Byzantines and crusaders were now damaged beyond repair. Villehardouin wrote, "Nor were they ever again as much at one as they had been before."[49]

The ruins were still smoldering when the emperor's expedition returned. It had been successful, and Alexius was so heartened by his people's loyalty that he fancied himself less dependent on the crusaders for military backing. According to Villehardouin, Alexius "thought he now had the upper hand [and] was

Letter of Justification

After the initial conquest of Constantinople, several leaders of the Fourth Crusade sent letters back to western Europe explaining what had taken place and—in their view—why. In one such letter, Count Hugh of Saint-Pol attempted to play down the financial rewards promised by Prince Alexius, writing instead that the crusaders were doing God's work:

We carried on the business of Jesus Christ with His help, to the point that the Eastern Church (whose head is Constantinople), along with the emperor and his entire empire reunited with its head, the Roman Pontiff . . . acknowledges itself to be the daughter of the Roman Church. It also wishes, with humbled head, to obey the same [the pope] more devoutly in the future—in accordance with normal custom. The patriarch [of Constantinople] himself, who desires and applauds this step, petitions all the way to the Roman See to receive the pallium [a white band] of his office and on this issue, he along with the emperor swore a sacred oath to us.

Indeed, the patriarch had agreed, but only reluctantly, to write to the pope acknowledging his supremacy. He never made the journey to Rome, however, and there was never any attempt to revise the practices of the Orthodox Church to comply with Roman Catholic custom.

Quoted in Jonathan Phillips, *The Fourth Crusade and the Sack of Constantinople.* New York: Viking, 2004, p. 195.

The writings of Geoffrey of Villehardouin, shown in crusader garb in this illustration, are valued as an example of medieval prose as well as a source of history.

filled with arrogance toward the barons."[50] His payments on his debt to the crusaders grew smaller and finally ceased altogether.

At the same time as the power and authority of Alexius increased, those of his father—the blind Isaac—diminished. The older co-emperor withdrew from public life and spent his days with self-proclaimed prophets and mystics.

The ill feeling in Constantinople erupted into violence again on December 1. A brawl broke out between a group of Byzantines and some Westerners—probably not crusaders, but merchants who had not yet left the city—and quickly became a riot. The Byzantine mob killed many Latins and took others prisoner, including women, children, and the elderly. These prisoners were slaughtered and their bodies burned.

Emboldened by their victory, the Byzantines commandeered some small boats and staged a surprise raid on the Venetian ships in the harbor. They were quickly routed by the Venetians, who pursued them to the city gates, killing many.

Ultimatum

With the city on the edge of open warfare, the crusaders finally decided on a face-to-face meeting with Alexius at which they planned to lay down an ultimatum. Six spokesmen, including Villehardouin, went to the imperial palace, swords at their sides. In contrast to previous visits, this was not a time for diplomatic niceties or flowery speeches. Speaking for the delegation, Conan of Bèthune bluntly reminded Alexius of services rendered to him and of his promises and demanded that those promises be fulfilled. If not, Conan said, "From this day forth [the crusaders] will not hold you as lord or friend, but will endeavor to obtain their due by all the means in their power."[51]

Before Alexius could answer, his courtiers erupted in anger. Never, they shouted, had any outsiders dared to speak so to the emperor. Seeing the Byzantines' "evil looks" and threatening gestures and thus feeling themselves in danger, the envoys left the throne room, mounted their horses, and left the city. "When they got outside the gate," Villehardouin wrote, "there was not one of them but felt glad of heart."[52]

Clari wrote in his memoir that Dandolo made one last personal appeal to Alexius, speaking from on board his galley to the emperor on shore. He renewed the demand for full payment. Alexius replied that he would do no more than had already been done. "Wretched boy," said the doge. "We dragged thee out of the filth . . . and into the filth we will cast thee again. And I defy thee, and I give thee well to know that I will do thee all the harm in my power from this moment forward."[53]

The War Begins

As Villehardouin wrote, "Thus did the war begin."[54] Once again, to the cru-

This painting of the attack on Constantinople shows the turmoil that reigned during medieval sieges. The city was besieged twice before being sacked.

saders it seemed they had no choice. It was the middle of winter and they were growing short of food and supplies. They did not have the money to continue the crusade. Their only options were to reconquer Constantinople or return to western Europe in disgrace.

The crusaders decided against an immediate all-out assault, however. The weather was cold and damp and, according to Clari, the Venetians said they could not properly rig their ships with flying bridges as before. Weeks thus passed with little more than constant skirmishing on both sides. The Byzantines repaired breaches in the city wall and, on January 1, sent fireships against the Venetian fleet.

Fireships were fearsome weapons that had been used in Mediterranean warfare for more than a thousand years. The object was to stuff old ships with combustible material and sail them under cover of darkness toward the enemy fleet. At the last possible moment, the fireships' crews would torch their ships and leap overboard, hoping that the blazing ships would set the enemy's vessels on fire. The Venetians, however, were skilled sailors. They swiftly got their ships under sail and, seizing the fireships with grappling hooks, towed them away from the main part of the fleet.

Short on Food

The crusaders, meanwhile, were short of food since they had been dependent on the city's residents for supplies. They ranged throughout the vicinity, Villehardouin wrote, "and what could be seized was seized."[55] It was not enough. Clari wrote that food was scarce in the crusader camp and that what food was available for sale brought high prices.

New Experiences

Constantinople was more exotic and more opulent than anything most of the members of the Fourth Crusade had ever seen. After they gained access to the city, the crusaders wandered the streets, taking in the sights. One such knight was Robert of Clari, who told this story of his comrades' wonder at what was, to them, a strange sight:

And while the barons were there at the palace, a king came there whose skin was all black, and he had a cross in the middle of his forehead that had been made with a hot iron. . . . When the emperor saw him coming, he rose to meet him and did great honor to him. And the emperor asked the barons: "Do you know," said he, "who this man is?" "Not at all, sire," said the barons. "I'faith," said the emperor, "this is the king of Nubia, who is come on pilgrimage to this city." . . . And they had an interpreter talk to him and ask him where his land was, and he answered . . . that his land was a hundred days' journey still beyond Jerusalem. . . . And he said that all the people of his land were Christians and that when a child was born and baptized they made a cross in the middle of his forehead with a hot iron, like the one he had. And the barons gazed at this king with great wonder.

Robert of Clari, *The Conquest of Constantinople*. Translated by Edgar Holmes McNeal. New York: W.W. Norton, 1936, pp. 79–80.

The scouring of the countryside angered the Byzantines, who urged their emperor to lead a major attack. Alexius, however, avoided a military confrontation with his former allies, causing Choniates to wonder if perhaps "he was siding with the [Byzantines] with his lips only and had inclined his hearts to the Latins."[56]

At this point the Byzantine Empire experienced a leadership crisis as factions backed various claimants to the throne. On January 25, Choniates wrote, the Byzantines' frustration "began to rise up in rebellion . . . like a boiling kettle . . . to blow off steam."[57] A mob seized the Hagia Sophia and forced the senators and chief clergy to gather for the purpose of selecting a new emperor. No one wanted the job, fearing that the crusaders would come to Alexius's defense. Finally, after three days of wrangling, a young noble, Nicholas Kannavos, was forced to accept the crown.

As predicted, Alexius turned to the crusaders, seeking forgiveness and renewing his promises. He dared not go to Boniface in person, fearing he might be seen and captured by his own subjects. Instead, he sent as his messenger his trusted chamberlain, a man named Alexius Dukas, known as Murtzuphulus, or "bushy-eyebrowed," because of this distinctive facial feature.

Murtzuphulus, who had become disenchanted with Alexius's favoritism toward the crusaders and secretly plotted against him, now saw a chance to overthrow the emperor. He delivered Alex-ius's message to Boniface as directed and then informed the leading Byzantine nobles of what he had done. The knowledge that the emperor had once again enlisted the aid of the crusaders swept away any of Alexius's remaining support.

Late that night, Murtzuphulus woke Alexius, pleading an emergency. The mob, he told the emperor, was on its way and he must flee. Still groggy with sleep, Alexius let himself be covered with a robe and escorted from the palace by Murtzuphulus's men, who promptly threw him into a dungeon. The next morning, Murtzuphulus was crowned Emperor Alexius V.

Four Emperors

There were now four emperors in Constantinople, but not for long. Isaac, in fact, might have already either died of natural causes or been murdered. Nicholas Kannavos still had the support of the faction that had gotten him crowned. Murtzuphulus, however, lured the leaders of this faction away with promises of high office. On February 2 Kannavos was arrested and was never seen again; most likely he was murdered.

That left Alexius IV. According to Choniates, Murtzuphulus twice forced him to drink poisoned wine, but both times the deposed emperor somehow managed to take an antidote and survive. Finally, Murtzuphulus went to Alexius's cell himself and strangled the man who had done so much to bring hardship on his people and city.

The Riches of Constantinople

There was nothing in western Europe to compare with Constantinople, and the ordinary knights of the Fourth Crusade were astounded by the richness of the churches they visited and the many holy relics they contained. Robert of Clari described the relics he saw in the Holy Chapel of the Boukoleon Palace:

One found there two pieces of the True Cross as large as the leg of a man and as long as half a *toise* [about 3 feet (0.9m)], and one found there also the iron of the lance with which Our Lord had His side pierced and two of the nails which were driven through His hands and feet, and one found there in a crystal phial quite a little of His blood, and one found there the tunic which He wore and which was taken from Him when they led Him to the Mount of Calvary, and one found there the blessed crown with which He was crowned, which was made of reeds with thorns as sharp as the points of daggers. And one found there a part of the robe of Our Lady [Mary] and the head of my lord St. John the Baptist and so many other rich relics that I could not recount them to you or tell you all the truth.

Robert of Clari, *The Conquest of Constantinople*. Translated by Edgar Holmes McNeal. New York: W.W. Norton, 1936, p. 103.

Like Alexius IV, Murtzuphulus refused to pay the money promised to the crusaders, making all-out war inevitable, but in any case the crusaders' objective had changed. Heretofore, their goal had been to continue the crusade by obtaining the money owed to them. Their attachment to Alexius or his capital city, however, had died with him. The way now seemed open for the conquest of Constantinople and the entire Byzantine Empire.

With this goal in mind, Dandolo, Boniface, and the French counts met and drew up what became known as the March Pact, an agreement specifying how not only the riches of Constantinople, but the empire as a whole would be apportioned if the city were conquered. Portable wealth—gold, silver, jewels, rich cloth—would be split three to one in favor of the Venetians up to the point at which all debts would be settled—about 200,000 silver marks. From then on, all would be divided equally between the French and the Venetians.

As for the city itself, the leaders agreed that, should it be captured, a group of twelve men—six Venetians and six from among the other crusaders —would select who would be crowned emperor. Whichever party—French or Venetian—got the throne, a member of the other would be named patriarch of the church.

Also, a second committee, this one numbering twelve Frenchmen and twelve Venetians, would parcel out to participants in the crusade the far-flung lands of the Byzantine Empire. The crusaders realized, of course, that there would be significant resistance and that some areas remained loyal to Alexius III, so they agreed to remain in Byzantium for an additional year to consolidate their gains before even considering continuing with the crusade. Finally, in what was to prove a masterpiece of irony, the leaders agreed that punishments of death or excommunication awaited those who despoiled churches or monasteries, sexually assaulted women, or kept booty for themselves without yielding it up for distribution.

The City's Defenses

Now, all that remained was to conquer the city, but the Byzantines and Murtzuphulus had not stood idly by. They had repaired and even strengthened the wall. The previous year's assault had broken many large chunks of masonry from the wall, and these now became weapons, to be thrown down on attackers or catapulted at ships. Wooden towers high atop the battlements were constructed to provide Byzantine soldiers with a better position from which to defend against the Venetians' flying bridges.

Constantinople was renowned for its size, splendor, and fortifications, as this sixteenth-century woodcut portrays. Breaching its walls took enormous courage and massive effort.

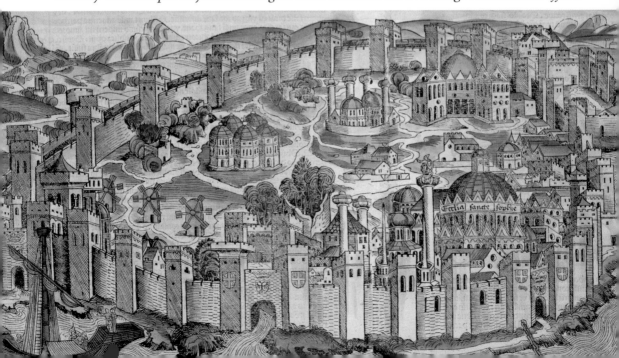

The crusaders likewise made ready and chose Friday, April 9, as the date of the assault. Instead of dividing their forces as before, the French and Venetians concentrated their attack on the wall directly across the Golden Horn from their camp. This was the same section captured by the Venetians the previous July.

This time, however, the assault went awry. A south wind, unusual in the Golden Horn, blew in the faces of the Venetian mariners, making it harder for their ships to approach the shore. Even when one of the flying bridges approached a tower, missiles hurled down from the new wooden superstructures prevented it from being secured. After several fruitless and costly hours, the crusaders abandoned the attack and retreated. The Byzantines on the walls hooted and jeered. Clari wrote that "some let down their clouts [pants] and showed them their backsides."[58]

Soul-Searching

The crusaders were demoralized by the defeat, wondering if it was a sign of divine displeasure. Seeing their discouragement, the clergy traveling with the crusaders resolved to convince the troops of the legitimacy of their cause and preached sermons throughout the camp on Sunday. They did not mention that the pope had expressly forbidden an attack on Constantinople, emphasizing instead that the Byzantines had rebelled and murdered their rightful ruler and

had not accepted the authority of the pope. Thus, they claimed, attacking the city "was not at all a sin, but rather a righteous deed."[59] The crusaders were thus convinced that theirs was a holy mission, and the diversion of the Fourth Crusade was complete. As Queller and Madden write, "From the crusaders' point of view, Jerusalem was now on the Bosporus."[60]

Meanwhile, the leaders decided to renew the assault on Monday with a change in tactics, two Venetian galleys attacking each tower instead of one. Hours into the second attack, however, it seemed the results would be the same as before. Then, as if in answer to the priests' sermons and the crusaders' prayers, the contrary wind shifted and the ships were able to maneuver close to the towers. Two ships, the *Paradise* and *Lady Pilgrim*, managed to attach their flying bridges to one of the towers.

The first man across, a Venetian, was killed, but the second, Andrew of Durebois, was better protected by his armor. Leaping onto the battlement, he fell to his hands and knees and, after withstanding several blows, stood and drew his sword. The astounded Byzantines fled, and the tower was taken.

Aleaumes of Clari

At about the same time a French nobleman, Pierre of Amiens, in whose company chronicler Robert of Clari fought, sought to smash through a bricked-up gate in the wall. Despite a rain of

Baldwin of Flanders triumphantly enters the reconquered Constantinople. This time Baldwin's spoils included being named emperor of Byzantium.

arrows, stones, and boiling tar, the company managed to hack an opening large enough for a man to crawl through. The first man to volunteer was Aleaumes of Clari, Robert's brother, who, although a priest, wore full armor and had taken an active part in combat.

Aleaumes ignored Robert's pleas to let someone else take the fearful risk. As Aleumes crawled through the hole, Robert tried to drag him back but was kicked aside. Once on the other side of the wall, Robert wrote, Aleaumes, miraculously unhit by stones from above, drew his sword, single-handedly charged the Byzantines, "and made them flee before him like cattle."[61]

Pierre and his force of about seventy men rapidly followed Aleaumes. Murtzuphulus, who had been directing the battle from a point very near the area of the breakthrough, quickly led a mounted charge toward the French force. The crusaders, although on foot, stood fast, Pierre urging them to "see to it that no one dare to give way, but think only to acquit yourselves well."[62] Faced with such determination, Murtzuphulus reacted as had Alexius III in July, retreating to his hilltop post.

Pierre's men ran to the nearest gate and opened it, allowing a horde of crusaders to pour through. When they charged toward Murtzuphulus's position,

the emperor and his troops, Choniates wrote, "took to their customary flight as the efficacious [most effective] medicine of salvation. . . . The enemy, now that there was no one to raise a hand against them, ran everywhere and drew the sword against every age and sex."[63]

End of the Battle

By now it was nearly sundown. The weary crusaders decided to make camp in the area where the wall had been breached. Alongside the weariness, however, was a sense of elation. "Never had they thought," Villehardouin wrote, "that in [even] a whole month they should be able to take the city, with its great churches, and great palaces, and the people that were in it."[64]

Many of those people did not remain for long, their emperor among them. During the night, Murtzuphulus slipped out of the city he had ruled for barely two months, took a small fishing boat, and sailed into the darkness.

Deciding that further resistance would be futile, the people of Constantinople went out the following morning to welcome their conquerors. They must have reckoned that, with their emperor fled and his troops either dead or departed, the worst would be over. They could not have been more wrong.

Chapter Six

THE CITY SACKED

While Constantinople had never before fallen to an outside enemy, upheavals from the inside had been all too frequent. Within the past year, six emperors had either died, been murdered, or fled. So, to the Byzantines, the day of April 13, 1204, seemed destined to bring just another change of rulers, even though the new rulers would be foreigners.

Accordingly, a large delegation of the leading citizens and priests went that morning to the crusader camp to convey the news of the emperor's flight and to acknowledge the man whom they reasoned would be their new emperor —Boniface of Montferrat. In a show of submission designed to spare the city any more bloodshed, Choniates wrote, the delegation "turned out to greet them [the crusaders] with crosses and venerable icons [symbolic portrayals] of Christ as was customary during festivals of solemn processions."[65]

The crusaders, however, schooled in the ferocity of Western warfare, had braced themselves for what they thought would be the first of perhaps many days of street-by-street fighting. Instead, advancing into the city on the morning after Murtzuphulus fled, they saw, instead of enemy soldiers brandishing swords, richly arrayed citizens and priests, making the sign of the cross and holding aloft pictures of Jesus, Mary, and various saints. If the Byzantines had hoped such a display would soften the hearts of their conquerors, they were very much mistaken. "Their disposition was not at all affected by what they saw," Choniates wrote, "nor did their lips break into the slightest smile, nor did the unexpected spectacle transform their grim and frenzied glance and fury into a semblance of cheerfulness."[66]

The Sack Begins

When it dawned on the crusaders that the city and all its wealth was theirs for the taking, they took it—in the most brutal manner possible. Starting with those who had come to them in peace, the crusaders fell on the people lining the streets and stripped them not only of their rich clothing and jewels, but also of the holy icons the people had thought would pacify them.

Thus began the sack of Constantinople —a three-day orgy of looting, killing, despoiling, and desecration so wide- spread that Choniates hardly knew how to begin describing it: "What then should I recount first and what last of those things dared at that time by these murderous men?"[67]

The pillaging began at the highest lev- els. Boniface hastened to take possession of the Boukoleon Palace, while Baldwin of Flanders seized the Blachernae Palace at the opposite end of the city. These palaces contained, Villehardouin wrote, treasure that "was so much that it was beyond all end or counting,"[68] and their new masters did not hesitate to appro-

Priceless treasures like this gilded icon and jewel-encrusted chalice were stolen or destroyed during the sack of Constantinople.

Acts of Outrage

Nicholas Mesarites, a priest and writer present in Constantinople at the time of its sacking by the crusaders, left this description of the conquerors' brutal search for wealth:

Breasts of women were [searched] to see whether a feminine ornament of gold was fastened to the body or hidden in them, hair was unloosed and head-coverings removed, and the homeless and moneyless dragged to the ground. Lamentation, moaning and woe were everywhere. Indecency was perpetrated, if any fair object was concealed within the recesses of the body; thus the ill-doers and mischief-makers abused nature itself. They slaughtered the new-born, killed prudent [matrons], stripped elder women, and outraged old ladies. They tortured the monks, they hit them with their fists and kicked their bellies, thrashing and rending their revered bodies with whips. Mortal blood was spilled on the holy altars, and on each, in place of the Lamb of God sacrificed for the salvation of the universe, many were dragged like sheep and beheaded, and on the holy tombs, the wretches slew innocents.

Quoted in Jonathan Phillips, *The Fourth Crusade and the Sack of Constantinople.* New York: Viking, 2004, p. 267.

priate it and place it under guard. As Baldwin later wrote, "So those who denied us small things have relinquished everything to us in divine judgment."[69]

The two palaces were occupied peacefully, the residents opening their doors to the invaders after obtaining promises that their lives would be spared. Others were not so fortunate. The leading crusaders spread throughout the city, historian Jonathan Phillips writes, "like a deadly virus running through the veins of a weak old man."[70] They barged into the richly furnished homes, stripping them of all wealth and frequently torturing the occupants to reveal where treasures might have been hidden.

"They exacted from all their money and chattel [goods], dwellings and clothing," Choniates wrote, "leaving to them nothing of all their goods."[71]

Crusader Greed

Such actions outraged not only the Byzantine historian, but also many of the lower-ranking crusaders, but for different reasons. Robert of Clari was disgusted that the "high men, the rich men" appropriated so much wealth for themselves without the knowledge of the ordinary knights or soldiers. "And from that time on," he wrote, "they began to betray the common people and to keep bad faith and bad comradeship with them."[72]

Constantinople, however, was a very large, very wealthy city, and Clari related that when the rank-and-file crusaders realized that the richest homes had been taken by their leaders, they made the best of things "and went each one and took what they could get. And many [houses] they found and many they took."[73]

One of the victims was Choniates himself. He was forced to flee from his home with members of his household, including his children and his pregnant wife. When he reached the massive walls of the city, he cursed them for not having kept the invaders out and cried out to his city, "What shall become of us? Whither shall we go? . . . When shall we look upon thee, not as thou now art, a plain of desolation and a valley of weeping?"[74]

Despoiling the Churches

Houses and palaces were by no means the only targets of the marauding crusaders. Much of the wealth of Constantinople was contained in churches, and the fact that these were Christian places of worship mattered not in the least to the crusaders. They smashed statuary and icons, ripped down curtains for their rich cloth, and demolished altars to get at the imbedded jewels. They snatched up cups and plates of gold and silver, discarding the bread and pouring out the wine that had been consecrated for communion. "Just as happened long ago, Christ was now disrobed and

Hovering cupolas adorn the ceiling of the Hagia Sophia in what is now Istanbul, Turkey.

mocked," Choniates wrote, " . . . and although his side was not pierced by the lance, yet once more streams of Divine Blood [symbolized by the wine] poured to the earth."[75]

Saddest of all to Choniates was the fate of the Hagia Sophia, holiest spot in the Byzantine Empire. The rampaging crusaders smashed the great altar of silver and gold, dividing the pieces among them. So vast was the treasure in the huge temple that the crusaders brought pack mules into the sanctuary to cart it all away. A prostitute, whom Choniates accused of also being a witch, sat in one of the chairs reserved for priests, sang a bawdy song, and did a lewd, high-kicking dance.

Churches were ransacked not only by the crusader soldiers, but also by the priests who ministered to their spiritual needs. The priests, however, were interested in the spiritual rather the than monetary value of what they looted. Many a golden plate or silver chalice would make its way from Constantinople to altars in France and Italy.

The Search for Relics

The real prizes for these ecclesiastical raiders, however, were relics—what were said to be body parts, clothing, or

other memorabilia of major Christian figures. One of the most brazen of the priests was Abbot Martin of Pairis. Gunther of Pairis recorded that his abbot "began to think also about his own booty and, lest he remain empty-handed while everyone else got rich, he resolved to use his own consecrated hands for pillage."[76] Martin invaded a monastery that he knew housed many relics. Finding an elderly monk, he drew a sword and threatened him with death unless he revealed the relics' hiding place. Martin stuffed as much inside his clothing as possible, then trudged back to his ship. When passers-by saw his bulging robes and asked what he carried, the abbot only smiled and replied, "We have done well."[77]

Works of art other than religious icons came in for their share of destruction. Marble statues, some from classical Greek and Roman times, were smashed. Libraries were ransacked, and how many works of classical poets and philosophers lost forever may never be known. Bronze statues were pulled down to be melted into coins, although Dandolo took the four huge horses from atop the Hippodrome chariot course and sent them to Venice, where they would remain on display even in the twenty-first century.

The People Brutalized

Yet even more violent than the crimes against property were those against people. Bands of crusaders, drunk on the spoils of Constantinople's wine cellars, attacked the citizens with no regard to age, sex, or infirmity. They ripped the clothing from women and girls and searched body cavities for hidden valuables. If the victims' male relatives tried to intervene, they were beaten or killed.

The crusaders' vow to respect the chastity of women in the conquered city was widely ignored. Nicholas Mesarites, a contemporary Byzantine priest and writer, told of them "tearing children from mothers and mothers from children, treating the virgin with wanton shame in holy chapels, viewing with fear neither the wrath of God nor the vengeance of man."[78] And Choniates wrote that "these madmen" spared no one—"pious matrons and girls of marriageable age or those maidens who, having chosen a life of chastity [as nuns], were consecrated to God."[79]

The crusade's leaders managed to bring the spree of violence and looting under some control after three days, but it was not until Sunday—Palm Sunday, as it happened—that it stopped. It was time then for the conquerors to give praise, Villehardouin wrote, for "all the honour that God had bestowed on them."[80]

The Collection

But the crusaders were eager to have something more tangible than honor bestowed on them. Accordingly, Boniface gave orders that all the wealth taken since the fall of the city would be amassed at designated churches, there

These bronze horses once sat atop Constantinople's hippodrome, or horse-racing stadium. They were removed to Venice by Doge Dandolo during the sack of the great city.

to be tallied before distribution. Once this was done, everyone was astounded at the amount, estimated by Villehardouin at 300,000 marks, or about $18 million—three and a half times the sum originally negotiated for passage by the French and Venetians. Clari wrote that "not since the world was made, was there ever seen or won so great a treasure."[81] Even Baldwin of Flanders, one of the wealthiest crusaders, claimed that the treasure constituted "such an inestimable abundance . . . that the entire Latin [western European] world does not seem to possess as much."[82]

However much the collected treasure was, the total was probably nowhere near the amount actually taken in the looting. Villehardouin admitted ruefully that, despite vows taken and at the risk of excommunication, many of the crusaders held back much of what they had seized. Some of the guilty were discovered and executed, including at least one knight, who was hanged with his shield around his neck as a sign of shame, but Villehardouin conceded that these were the minority. He estimated that 500,000 marks' worth of treasure, about $30 million, was kept by those who had taken it.

Furthermore, according to Clari, much of the wealth that was surrendered seemed to vanish before it could be distributed. He wrote that twenty French and Venetian knights thought to be most trustworthy were selected to stand guard over the hoard, but that "the very ones who were to guard the wealth took gold ornaments and whatever else they wanted and robbed the treasure."[83] So greedy were the guards,

The Pope's Reaction

Pope Innocent III, who had forbidden the crusaders to attack Constantinople and who threatened to excommunicate any who disobeyed him, was astounded to learn not only that the city had been taken, but that it had been brutally sacked. In a letter to his personal representative on the crusade, Peter Capuano, the pope despaired of there ever being peace or accord between the Byzantines and the West:

How, indeed, is the Greek church to be brought back into ecclesiastical union and to a devotion for the Apostolic See when she has been beset with so many afflictions and persecutions that she sees in the Latins only an example of perdition and the works of darkness, so that she now, and with reason, detests the Latins more than dogs? As for those who were supposed to be seeking the ends of Jesus Christ, not their own ends,

whose swords, which they were supposed to use against the pagans, are now dripping with Christian [blood. They] have spared neither age nor sex. They have committed incest, adultery, and fornication before the eyes of men. They have exposed both matrons and virgins, even those dedicated to God, to the sordid lusts of boys. Not satisfied with breaking open the imperial treasury and plundering the goods of princes and lesser men, they also laid their hands on the treasures of the churches and, what is more serious, on their very possessions. They have even ripped silver plates from the altars and have hacked them to pieces among themselves. They violated the holy places and have carried off crosses and relics.

Innocent III, Reprimand of Papal Legate, in *Internet Medieval Sourcebook*, Paul Halsell, editor. www.fordham.edu/halsall/source/1204innocent.html..

he wrote, that virtually all the gold and precious gems disappeared, with only the silver remaining.

The Division

What remained was divided according to class. Each knight received twenty marks (about $1,200), each mounted common soldier and each member of the clergy ten marks, and each foot soldier five marks. The ordinary knights and soldiers, who had seen for themselves the extent of the city's wealth, were indignant and suspected that they had been cheated. Clari was especially offended that his brother Aleaumes, whose courage and audacity had contributed so much to the victory, would receive only a clergyman's share. Count Hugh of Saint-Pol intervened on Aleaumes's behalf, ruling he would get a knight's share since he had done more than "any one of three hundred knights."[84]

The next order of business was to choose the new emperor. The Byzantines expected Boniface to mount the throne, and the marquis himself wanted the crown, but there were other candidates such as Baldwin of Flanders and Louis of Blois. Dandolo was mentioned, but the doge's age was against him. Moreover, given the subtlety with which he had always done business, he probably was able to accomplish more on Venice's behalf from behind the scenes.

As provided by the March Pact, twelve electors were chosen—six from Venice and six from France. This choice was easy for the Venetians, who were used to making decisions by committee, and particularly since no Venetian was a contender for the emperor's crown. There was considerable squabbling, however, among the French, Germans, and Italians, all of whom preferred electors who would back their respective favorites for emperor. At length, however, six churchmen were selected and, after a special mass to seek spiritual guidance, the electors were locked into a chapel to begin their deliberations.

The New Emperor

There is no record of exactly how long the electors deliberated, but the bishop of Soissons finally emerged to announce a decision he said was unanimous. "Lords, we are agreed, let God be thanked! upon the choice of an emperor," the bishop said to the anxiously waiting assembly, "and you have all sworn that he whom we shall elect as emperor shall be held by you to be emperor indeed, and that if any one gainsay [oppose] him, you will be his helpers. And we name him now . . . the Count Baldwin of Flanders."[85]

According to Choniates, Baldwin's election had been engineered by Dandolo, who did not want Boniface as emperor because the marquis's home base was in northern Italy, much nearer to Venice than was Flanders. Dandolo wanted to make certain, Choniates wrote, that "should the emperor and the Venetians ever have a falling out, the

Murtzuphulus's Fate

Emperor Alexius V, better known by his nickname of Murtzuphulus, fled from Constantinople after its capture by the crusaders. Less than a year later, he was blinded by his father-in-law and handed over to the new rulers of the city. Niketas Choniates recorded what happened to him:

He was brought to trial for having seized his lord and emperor and put him to death by strangulation. His defense was that he looked upon the emperor as a traitor to his country who justly deserved his punishment, not only he alone for the crimes he had committed but others as well, as many partisans and kinsmen who had joined him. But no heed was paid to the words he had spoken, and the Latins refused to lend an attentive ear to the further arguments of this anguished man who was then condemned to an unprecedented and most violent death: placing him atop the lofty column standing in the Forum of the Bull, the Latins cast him down; falling feet first and then tumbling headlong, he shortly crashed aslant and died a most pitiable death.

Niketas Choniates, *O City of Byzantium: Annals of Niketas Choniates.* Translated by Harry J. Magoulias. Detroit: Wayne State University Press, 1984, p. 334.

---

emperor would not be able to summon his greater forces from nearby and easily penetrate Venice's borders."[86]

So it was that on May 9 there occurred an event that few could have forecast—a Flemish count assumed the title that could be traced back more than twelve hundred years to Augustus Caesar. In a letter to Pope Innocent, Baldwin attributed everything to God's

Venice's Doge Dandolo crowns Count Baldwin of Flanders as the first Western emperor of the Byzantine Empire, renamed the Latin Empire of Constantinople.

will: "Divine Clemency has performed a wondrous turn of events round about us . . . there can be no doubt, even among the unbelievers, but that the hand of the Lord guided all of these events, since nothing that we hoped for or previously anticipated occurred."[87]

The Byzantine view of the righteousness of the Fourth Crusade was understandably different. "In truth," Choniates wrote, the crusaders "were exposed as frauds. Seeking to avenge the Holy Sepulcher, they raged openly against Christ and sinned by overturning the Cross with the cross they bore on their backs, not even shuddering to trample on it for the sake of a little gold and silver."[88]

Epilogue

Aftermath and Consequences

The immediate result of the Fourth Crusade was the establishment of what historians call the Latin Empire of Constantinople. The empire was to be short-lived—barely half a century. The long-term consequences of the crusade, however, would be far-reaching, extending even to the present day.

Even though many of the crusaders still hoped to continue to Jerusalem, this original intent was abandoned. The new emperor needed his troops to consolidate the victory. Accordingly, the pope's representative in Constantinople, Peter Capuano, released the crusaders—but without Pope Innocent's knowledge and to his great anger when he learned of it—from their vows to retake the Holy Land if they would remain one year.

Shortly after Baldwin's coronation, the victors began to carve up the old empire. Venice got the areas most advantageous to her trading interests—the western coast of the Greek peninsula, ports in southern Greece, and ports on the Sea of Marmara. Boniface established the kingdom of Thessalonica in central and northern Greece. He also laid claim to the bulk of present-day Turkey, although this area was effectively controlled by the Turks, and Boniface never really attempted to impose his authority there.

Baldwin, as emperor, was to rule over Constantinople and Thrace—the European part of the Byzantine empire extending westward around the Aegean Sea to the Danube River. Most of that region, however, remained loyal to either Alexius III or Murtzuphulus. Baldwin set out to conquer it, but was taken captive in a battle against the Byzantines and their Bulgarian allies at the Thracian city of Adrianople in 1205 and later executed.

Pope Innocent III (far left) is famed for approving the new religious orders of Franciscans and Dominicans (shown here), but his goals for the Fourth Crusade failed miserably.

Baldwin was succeeded by his younger brother, Henry, who proved to be an effective ruler and was able to bring most of Thrace under his control. After he died in 1216, however, a string of ineffectual rulers diminished the power of the Latin Empire to a point where, in 1261, it was easily defeated by the Byzantines.

Religious Failure

The Latin Empire was a religious as well as a political failure. Pope Innocent III had high hopes that the crusaders, even though they had disobeyed him, might have succeeded in uniting Christendom. Despite his anger over the sack of Constantinople, he never followed through on his threat of excommunicating the crusaders and never suggested that they withdraw from the city. Instead, he took the view that God had seen fit to punish "an evil people," for "who can know the mind of the Lord?"[89]

Innocent's hopes of a united Christendom were soon dashed, however. First, against his wishes and without his approval, a Venetian was elected patriarch of Constantinople. Innocent had never forgiven the Venetians for—in his view —corrupting the crusade and thought this was another way for them to avoid papal authority. More important, however, was the general antagonism of the conquered people to their conquerors' religion. The people steadfastly refused to give up the practices of the Eastern church. When the pope tried to force new bishops promoted from within the local population to be consecrated according to Western rites, they declined.

The religious divide, however, was more profound than rites, or even authority. Innocent had been correct when he wrote that the brutal sack of Constantinople would work against unification. Steven Runciman, one of the most noted historians of the Crusades, wrote, "It [the division of Christendom] went deeper: it was based on mutual dislike between the peoples of Eastern and Western Christendom."[90] Indeed, the Fourth Crusade left a scar on the relationship between the two branches of Christianity that still has not healed. As recently as 2000, an American writer and member of the Greek Orthodox church, Nicholas Cooke, concluded an essay on the crusade by writing, "Scientists tell us that Venice slowly is sinking into the Adriatic. It deserves to do so. Perhaps it is trying to hide from its sins."[91]

Winners

There were some "winners" in the Fourth Crusade. Certainly some of the high-ranking crusaders emerged wealthy,

especially if Robert of Clari was correct in charging that they had helped themselves to a large part of the treasure before anything was divided. Many of the ordinary knights and soldiers, however, probably had little to show for the three or four years they spent away from home.

Venice undoubtedly got more out of the Fourth Crusade than anyone. Much of Constantinople's wealth would be dispersed throughout France, Germany, and northern Italy, but Venice's considerable share was consolidated in the city. Venice was thus enriched not only by money, but also by holy relics and works of art.

Moreover, the republic's acquisition of key ports in the eastern Mediterranean made it the dominant force in trade. It was thus strengthened to the extent that it later was able to defeat its archrival, Genoa, for control of the Mediterranean.

Losers

The Byzantines, although they eventually recovered their capital, were losers in the long run. The crusaders had dealt the empire a blow from which it never recovered. It became progressively weaker until, in 1453, the cannons of the Ottoman Turks battered Constantinople into submission. The entire Middle East and Asia Minor were now in Muslim hands, and Christians became a small, often persecuted minority.

The Muslims did not stop at Constantinople, but fought their way west-

At one time Constantinople's Hagia Sophia was one of the grandest churches in Christendom. Today it is a great mosque in the modern city of Istanbul.

ward, halted only at the gates of Vienna, Austria. Still, much of eastern Europe became Muslim, and in areas where Christians and Muslims coexisted, religious conflict continued for centuries, most recently in Croatia and Bosnia.

Some scholars think that Muslim expansion might have been stopped, or at least slowed, had western Europeans supported the Byzantine Empire rather than tearing it apart. Nineteenth-century British historian Edwin Pears wrote, "Constantinople had been for centuries the strongest bulwark of defense against Asia. The men of the West had every interest to maintain and to strengthen it. Instead of doing so, they virtually let loose Asia upon Europe."[92]

But perhaps the greatest loser as a result of the sack of Constantinople has been humanity itself. Irretrievably lost was the priceless legacy of a proud civilization, the direct heir of the Roman Empire. The so-called Queen of Cities had been violated and her crown trampled underfoot. Visitors to today's Constantinople—Istanbul—see a mighty city, but the wonders that awed Robert of Clari and his compatriots have mostly vanished. Slightly more than one hundred years after the city was sacked, the Arab geographer Abulfeda viewed the ruins and sadly noted the fields where temples and palaces once stood. "It is clear," he lamented, "that, once upon a time when Constantinople was in its pristine state, it was among the noblest cities in the world."[93]

Notes

Introduction: East and West

1. W.B. Bartlett, *An Ungodly War: The Sack of Constantinople and the Fourth Crusade.* Phoenix Mill, UK: Sutton, 2000, p. xvii.

Chapter 1: "God Wills It!"

2. Quoted in Jonathan Phillips, *The Fourth Crusade and the Sack of Constantinople.* New York: Viking, 2004, p. 13.
3. William of Malmesbury, *Gesta Regum Anglorum: The History of the English Kings.* Translated by A.B. Mynors, R.M. Thompson, and M. Winterbottom. Oxford, UK: Clarendon Press, 1998, p. 655.

Chapter 2: Call to Arms

4. Quoted in Bartlett, *Ungodly War,* p. 49.
5. Quoted in Phillips, *Fourth Crusade and the Sack of Constantinople,* p. 27.
6. Quoted in Phillips, *Fourth Crusade and the Sack of Constantinople,* pp. 35, 37.
7. Quoted in Geoffrey of Villehardouin, *Chronicle of the Fourth Crusade and the Conquest of Constantinople,* in *Internet Medieval Sourcebook,* Paul Halsall, editor. www.fordham.edu/halsall/basis/villehardouin.html.
8. Quoted in Villehardouin, *Chronicle of the Fourth Crusade.*
9. Villehardouin, *Chronicle of the Fourth Crusade.*
10. Villehardouin, *Chronicle of the Fourth Crusade.*
11. Quoted in Villehardouin, *Chronicle of the Fourth Crusade.*
12. Villehardouin, *Chronicle of the Fourth Crusade.*
13. Villehardouin, *Chronicle of the Fourth Crusade.*

Chapter 3: Diversions

14. Villehardouin, *Chronicle of the Fourth Crusade.*
15. Quoted in Phillips, *Fourth Crusade and the Sack of Constantinople,* p. 85.
16. Donald E. Queller and Thomas F. Madden, *The Fourth Crusade: The Conquest of Constantinople.* Philadelphia: University of Pennsylvania Press, 1997, p. 37.
17. Robert of Clari, *The Conquest of Constantinople.* Translated by Edgar Holmes McNeal. New York: W.W. Norton, 1936, p. 39.
18. Villehardouin, *Chronicle of the Fourth Crusade.*

19. Villehardouin, *Chronicle of the Fourth Crusade.*

20. Quoted in Villehardouin, *Chronicle of the Fourth Crusade.*

21. Clari, *Conquest of Constantinople,* p. 42.

22. Villehardouin, *Chronicle of the Fourth Crusade.*

23. Quoted in Villehardouin, *Chronicle of the Fourth Crusade.*

24. Quoted in Clari, *Conquest of Constantinople,* p. 44.

25. Villehardouin, *Chronicle of the Fourth Crusade.*

26. Quoted in Clari, *Conquest of Constantinople,* p. 59.

27. Villehardouin, *Chronicle of the Fourth Crusade.*

28. Villehardouin, *Chronicle of the Fourth Crusade.*

29. Villehardouin, *Chronicle of the Fourth Crusade.*

Chapter 4: The City Conquered

30. Villehardouin, *Chronicle of the Fourth Crusade.*

31. Niketas Choniates, *O City of Byzantium: Annals of Niketas Choniates.* Translated by Harry J. Magoulias. Detroit: Wayne State University Press, 1984, p. 252.

32. Choniates, *O City of Byzantium,* p. 296.

33. Quoted in Villehardouin, *Chronicle of the Fourth Crusade.*

34. Clari, *Conquest of Constantinople,* p. 70.

35. Quoted in Villehardouin, *Chronicle of the Fourth Crusade.*

36. Choniates, *O City of Byzantium,* p. 298.

37. Choniates, *O City of Byzantium,* p. 299.

38. Villehardouin, *Chronicle of the Fourth Crusade.*

39. Villehardouin, *Chronicle of the Fourth Crusade.*

40. Choniates, *O City of Byzantium,* p. 299.

41. Choniates, *O City of Byzantium,* p. 299.

42. Choniates, *O City of Byzantium,* p. 302.

43. Choniates, *O City of Byzantium,* p. 302.

44. Quoted in Phillips, *Fourth Crusade and the Sack of Constantinople,* p. 198.

45. Quoted in Villehardouin, *Chronicle of the Fourth Crusade.*

46. Villehardouin, *Chronicle of the Fourth Crusade.*

Chapter 5: The City Reconquered

47. Clari, *Conquest of Constantinople,* p. 70.

48. Choniates, *O City of Byzantium,* p. 303–304.

49. Villehardouin, *Chronicle of the Fourth Crusade.*

50. Villehardouin, *Chronicle of the Fourth Crusade.*

51. Quoted in Villehardouin, *Chronicle of the Fourth Crusade.*

52. Villehardouin, *Chronicle of the Fourth Crusade.*
53. Quoted in Clari, *Conquest of Constantinople*, p. 84.
54. Villehardouin, *Chronicle of the Fourth Crusade.*
55. Villehardouin, *Chronicle of the Fourth Crusade.*
56. Choniates, *O City of Byzantium*, p. 307.
57. Choniates, *O City of Byzantium*, p. 307.
58. Clari, *Conquest of Constantinople*, p. 93.
59. Clari, *Conquest of Constantinople*, p. 94.
60. Queller and Madden, *Fourth Crusade*, p. 174.
61. Clari, *Conquest of Constantinople*, p. 98.
62. Clari, *Conquest of Constantinople*, p. 98.
63. Choniates, *O City of Byzantium*, p. 313.
64. Villehardouin, *Chronicle of the Fourth Crusade.*

Chapter 6: The City Sacked

65. Choniates, *O City of Byzantium*, p. 314.
66. Choniates, *O City of Byzantium*, p. 314.
67. Choniates, *O City of Byzantium*, p. 314.
68. Villehardouin, *Chronicle of the Fourth Crusade.*
69. Quoted in Phillips, *Fourth Crusade and the Sack of Constantinople*, p. 259.
70. Phillips, *Fourth Crusade and the Sack of Constantinople*, p. 259.
71. Choniates, *O City of Byzantium*, p. 316.
72. Clari, *Conquest of Constantinople*, p. 100.
73. Clari, *Conquest of Constantinople*, p. 101.
74. Choniates, *O City of Byzantium*, p. 325.
75. Choniates, *O City of Byzantium*, p. 315.
76. Quoted in Queller and Madden, *Fourth Crusade*, p. 195.
77. Quoted in Phillips, *Fourth Crusade and the Sack of Constantinople*, p. 262.
78. Quoted in Phillips, *Fourth Crusade and the Sack of Constantinople*, p. 264.
79. Choniates, *O City of Byzantium*, p. 315.
80. Villehardouin, *Chronicle of the Fourth Crusade.*
81. Clari, *Conquest of Constantinople*, p. 101.
82. Quoted in Phillips, *Fourth Crusade and the Sack of Constantinople*, p. 268.
83. Clari, *Conquest of Constantinople*, p. 101.
84. Clari, *Conquest of Constantinople*, p. 118.
85. Quoted in Villehardouin, *Chronicle of the Fourth Crusade.*

86. Choniates, *O City of Byzantium*, p. 328.
87. Quoted in Phillips, *Fourth Crusade and the Sack of Constantinople*, p. 275.
88. Choniates, *O City of Byzantium*, p. 316.

Epilogue: Aftermath and Consequences

89. Quoted in Phillips, *Fourth Crusade and the Sack of Constantinople*, p. 303.
90. Quoted in Michael Angold, *The Fourth Crusade*. Harlow, UK: Longman, 2003, p. 189.
91. Nicholas A. Cooke, *The Sack of Constantinople*. Church History with a Focus on Orthodoxy. http://aggreen.net/church_history/1204_sack.html.
92. Quoted in Ernle Bradford, *The Sundered Cross*. Englewood Cliffs, NJ: Prentice Hall, 1967, p. 197.
93. Quoted in Bradford, *Sundered Cross*, p. 202.

Chronology

1095–99
First Crusade

1145–49
Second Crusade

1187
Muslims under Saladin capture Jerusalem

1189–92
Third Crusade

1195
Alexius III deposes Isaac as emperor in Constantinople

1198
June: Pope Innocent III launches Fourth Crusade

1199
November: Thibaut of Champagne and Louis of Blois commit to crusade at tournament at Écry

1201
April: Crusaders and Doge Dandolo sign Treaty of Venice

August: Boniface of Montferrat becomes leader of crusade after death of Thibaut

1202
October: Crusaders sail from Venice

November: Crusaders besiege and capture city of Zara

December: Envoys from Prince Alexius of Constantinople arrive in Zara to seek crusaders' help

1203
June 23: Crusade arrives at Constantinople

July 17–18: Crusaders attack Constantinople; Alexius III flees; Isaac is reinstated as emperor

August 1: Prince Alexius becomes co-emperor as Alexius IV

1204
January: Byzantines attack crusader fleet with fireships

January 27–28: Murtzuphulus imprisons Alexius IV, who is later murdered

March: French and Venetians sign agreement on division of Byzantine Empire

April 9: Byzantines repulse initial attack on Constantinople

April 12: Crusaders capture Constantinople

April 13–15: Crusaders sack Constantinople

May 16: Baldwin of Flanders is crowned emperor of the Latin Empire of Byzantium

1261
Byzantines recapture Constantinople; Latin Empire ends

For Further Reading

Books

Timothy L. Biel, *The Crusades*. San Diego: Lucent, 1995. Comprehensive account of the background, events, and consequences of the Crusades.

John Davenport, *Saladin*. Philadelphia: Chelsea House, 2003. The life and impact of the ruler and warrior who led Muslim troops during and after the Third Crusade.

Craig A. and Katherine M. Doherty, *King Richard the Lionhearted and the Crusades*. Berkeley Heights, NJ: Enslow, 2002. This addition to the World History series gives an account of the adventures and misadventures of King Richard I of England during the Third Crusade.

Michael J. O'Neal, *The Crusades: Almanac*. Detroit: UXL, 2005. Part of a three-volume set, this entry discusses the conquering of Jerusalem, pilgrimages to the Holy Land, the traditions of chivalry, Shiite and Sunni Muslims, and territorial expansion and colonization as motivations for the Crusades.

Web Sites

Rachel Gilberts, Middle Ages, www.mnsu.edu/emuseum/history/middleages/. Fun-to-explore and extremely well illustrated site on the Middle Ages. Produced by Minnesota State University at Mankato.

Paul Halsall, editor, Internet Medieval Sourcebook, www.fordham.edu/halsall/sbook.html. A comprehensive collection of primary sources from the Middle Ages, including substantial materials on the Crusades.

Skip Knox, *The Fourth Crusade*. http://crusades.boisestate.edu/4th/. This part of a Boise State University professor's online course on the Crusades tells the story of the Fourth Crusade in short, easy-to-read segments.

NetSERF: The Internet Connection to the Middle Ages, www.netserf.org. Provides links to hundreds of aspects of life in the Middle Ages, including biographies, art, architecture, literature, and culture.

Middle Ages, www.learner.org/exhibits/middleages/. Extensive site on different facets of Middle Ages culture produced by Annenberg CPB/Learner. org.

Index

Picture Credits

Cover: Palazzo Ducale, Venice, Italy/Bridgeman Art Library
akg-images, 53
© Bettmann/CORBIS, 65
Bibliotheque Municipale de Lyon, France/The Bridgeman Art
     Library, 58
Bibliotheque Nationale, Paris, France, Archives Charmet/
     The Bridgeman Art Library, 20
Bibliotheque Nationale, Paris, France, Giraudon/The Bridgeman
     Art Library, 33
Cameraphoto/Art Resource, NY, 47, 84
Chateau de Versailles, France, Giraudon/The Bridgeman Art
     Library, 40
Erich Lessing/Art Resource, NY, 55, 81
Hermitage, St. Petersburg, Russia/The Bridgeman Art Library, 11
© Historical Picture Archive/CORBIS, 71
Mary Evans Picture Library, 73
Maury Aaseng, 52
Musee Conde, Chantilly, France, Giraudon/The Bridgeman
     Art Library, 87
Museo Lazaro Galdiano, Madrid, Spain, Lauros/Giraudon/The
     Bridgeman Art Library, 42
Palazzo Ducale, Venice, Italy/The Bridgeman Art Library, 67
North Wind Pictures, 23, 27, 32
Scala/Art Resource, NY, 19, 34, 37
Snark/Art Resource, NY, 16
The Art Archive/Biblioteca Nazionale Palermo/Dagli Orti, 13
The Art Archive/Bodleian Library Oxford, 48
The Art Archive/Dagli Orti, 79
Victoria & Albert Museum, London/Art Resource, NY, 89
Werner Forman/Art Resource, NY, 76 (left and right)

About the Author

William W. Lace is a native of Fort Worth, Texas, where he is executive assistant to the chancellor at Tarrant County College. He holds a bachelor's degree from Texas Christian University, a master's degree from East Texas State, and a doctorate from the University of North Texas. Before joining Tarrant County College, he was director of the news service at the University of Texas at Arlington and a writer and columnist for the *Fort Worth Star-Telegram*. He has written more than twenty-five books for Lucent, one of which—*The Death Camps*—was selected by the New York Public Library for its 1999 Recommended Teenage Reading List. He and his wife, Laura, a retired school librarian, live in Arlington, Texas, and have two children and three grandchildren.

DATE DUE

FOLLETT